ENGLISH AS A FOREIGN LANGUAGE
History, Development, and Methods of Teaching

University of Oklahoma Press : *Norman*

ENGLISH AS A FOREIGN LANGUAGE

History, Development, and Methods of Teaching

By

STEVEN G. DARIAN

INTERNATIONAL STANDARD BOOK NUMBER: 0–8061–1005–8

LIBRARY OF CONGRESS CATALOG CARD NUMBER: 76–177332

To my parents
A debt lovingly repaid

Preface

THIS BOOK has grown out of many years' experience teaching English as a foreign language in the United States and overseas. It is offered as a guide, a means of determining linguistically sound approaches, amidst the endless pronouncements on language teaching. I have tried to strike a balance between theory and practice, keeping always in mind the needs of the language teacher and the foreign-language program, in their immediate and long-term contexts.

Many people's thoughts and suggestions have made this book possible—there are no true beginnings. I would especially like to thank Professors Robert Fowkes and Louise Gurren of New York University and Professor Sumner Ives of the City University of New York, for their helpful comments. I would also like to thank the Research Council of Rutgers University for encouragement and support of the project.

STEVEN G. DARIAN

Camden, New Jersey
July 15, 1971

Contents

ENGLISH AS A FOREIGN LANGUAGE
History, Development, and Methods of Teaching

❦ I ❧

Introduction

WITH THE EMERGENCE of English as the first medium of international communication, a great many people in America and overseas have entered the field of English as a foreign language (EFL). New York, Florida, and Texas offer considerable programs for Spanish-speaking people. In the federal government alone, seven agencies are concerned with EFL teaching.* During the period 1955–63 the Agency for International Development allocated $17 million for English language programs. A 1963 survey revealed over 1,900 teachers involved in United States government-sponsored EFL projects, with a 1967–68 projection above 4,065. In 1961, 221,000 students were enrolled in United States Information Service (USIS) English classes overseas, an 11 per cent increase over the preceding year.

In the United States, English is taught to thousands of

* These include the Departments of State, Defense, Health, Education, and Welfare, and Interior, the Agency for International Development, the United States Information Agency, and the Peace Corps. See Francis J. Colligan, "The English Language—A Growing Export," in Virginia French Allen (ed.), *On Teaching English to Speakers of Other Languages*, Part I, p. 13.

foreign visitors at colleges and universities. Furthermore, two-thirds of the roughly 90,000 foreign students come from non-English-speaking countries and are studying EFL at more than fifty colleges and universities.

This tremendous expansion of the field has developed spasmodically as a response to different historical stimuli: the late-nineteenth-century immigration of non-English-speaking people, the rise of structural linguistics in the late 1920's, and, especially since World War II, the need for English as a technical language in emerging nations.

Because of the exploding research in applied linguistics over the last thirty years, a great variety of materials and teaching methods have come into use, some reflecting new and others older theories of language teaching. Certain approaches work best with large groups, others with smaller classes; certain techniques work best with beginning classes, and others with intermediate or advanced levels. Since more work has been done by American linguists on EFL than on any single foreign language, this study should have direct application to methods, materials, and general design of programs for all foreign languages. A study examining the development of English as a foreign language and a discussion of applied linguistics and language teaching theory should prove valuable for all those concerned with language teaching.

Although EFL teaching has engaged Americans almost since the founding of the country, it did not appear as a major problem until the late nineteenth and early twentieth centuries with the ever increasing immigration of non-English-speaking people. Even so, integrated university programs for foreign students were not established until the 1940's. The English Language Institute of the University of Michigan, which pioneered in EFL research, did not open its doors until 1941, while well-known programs such as those at New York University and Columbia were not fully established until 1948 and 1950. However, EFL courses were taught in colleges and at every level of education, public and private, long before then. Special English courses for foreigners were offered through public schools in Pennsylvania as early as 1842.

There is no single formula in language teaching. I have particular preferences, but people and situations differ. This discussion of linguistically sound approaches ancient and modern offers the reader a rich provender to choose from in evolving his own system, one that is rigorous and yet allows for his own individual form of expression. Throughout the study I have attempted to show the relationship between modern practice and some of the more prescient writers on language teaching from earlier times. Tracing the evolution of certain language-teaching theories should enable the reader better to understand and evaluate these theories and their place in the modern language program. In the space available I have also tried to outline those contributions made to foreign language teaching by the applications of phonology and other levels of structural linguistics, including morphology and syntax, and the implications of transformation-generative grammar for the teaching of English as a foreign language. A final section will touch on problems and potentials of EFL teaching overseas.

❧ II ❧

The Historical Background of Linguistics and Language Teaching Before 1880

THE MOST FAMOUS language teacher of antiquity was Marcus Fabius Quintilian, born in Spain soon after the start of the Christian Era (A.D. 35–95). At a young age he went to Rome, where, after a dutiful apprenticeship, he became an advocate and teacher of rhetoric. His text, the *Institutio Oratoria*, reflects his experience as a teacher of rhetoric in Rome for twenty years and sums up "all that was valuable in countless handbooks of rhetoric which had appeared during the previous century."[1]

According to Quintilian, the first medium of instruction for a Roman boy should be Greek, since the student will acquire Latin naturally in his daily course of events. Further, he says that the Latin language is derived from the Greek,[2] an etymological blunder for which the great teacher must be forgiven. At any rate, the student should be placed under the charge of a native speaker of Greek.

Concerning language-teaching methodology, Quintilian makes the following suggestions: (1) an Aesop fable is read aloud and the student is asked to tell the story in his own words; (2) later he is supposed to write down the story in simple language; (3) the student paraphrases in prose a passage read in class from a poet; (4) then he writes a short composition on a proverb or saying of a great man.

In dealing with spelling and pronunciation, the author urges that except in cases where usage is firmly established, every word should be written the way it is pronounced. "For the function of letters is to preserve our utterances. . . ."[3]

As for choosing correct forms, Quintilian regards custom as the surest guide to proper usage. "To retain words that are obsolete and disused, is a species impertinence. . . . It would be almost ridiculous to prefer the language which men have spoken rather than that which they now speak."[4] In addition, he suggests it is not the usage of the common man that should be sought; "for if custom be merely termed that which the greater number do, it will furnish a most dangerous rule, not only for language, but what is of greater importance, for life. For where is there so much virtue that what is right can please the majority. . . . Custom in speaking, therefore, I shall call the agreement of the educated."[5] This is Quintilian's greatest contribution to modern language teaching: the concept that correctness derives from the usage of the educated. Such a concept underwent slow and often painful development through Erasmus in the sixteenth century to Joseph Priestly in the eighteenth and Samuel Kirkham in the nineteenth. It provided the basis for Charles Fries's significant study of English syntax, *American English Grammar*, and has come to play an important part in determining standards of usage in modern foreign language teaching, especially in the teaching of English as a foreign language.

Until the sixteenth century, authors of foreign language texts assumed that the only thing necessary for the description of a language was to list paradigms of inflections for each of the parts of speech, supply a lexicon, and give the rules for arranging the words in a sentence. There was no treatment of phonology.[6] In the sixteenth century, there began to appear textbooks containing short dialogues representing typical conversations published in parallel columns with translations. At the same time, several leading educational figures emerged to give new shape and direction to language teaching.

One of the most important was Desiderius Erasmus (1466–1536), the great Dutch scholar who was influenced considerably by Quintilian. Erasmus "knew Quintilian from end to end, and built up his own work on education on that foundation."[7] Like Quintilian, he assumed that grammar and rhetoric were a means and the goal "eloquence," which to Erasmus meant development of the critical powers combined with wide learning and moral virtue to produce the educated man. This process, in addition to rhetoric, required long training in composition and speaking.[8] To Erasmus, language was a body of phenomena whose laws were discernible by study of the given facts, namely the language itself. Once discovered, these laws could be used for speech and interpretation. The author rules out a priori assumption on usage, since language itself is but generalized usage.

According to Erasmus, education begins unconsciously. Speech—that is, Latin—should be acquired as early as possible, preferably with a private teacher. Very little formal grammar should be presented at first. The student should be given historical and mythological stories, descriptions of plant and animal life, and so forth, all illustrated by pictures. Instead of formal grammar, Erasmus urges the use of *Colloquies*, a collection of dialogues on incidents of daily life. Reading is next in the order of importance, followed by writing.

After gaining mastery over grammar and the ability to vary and expand words and phrases, the student practices imitating models. In the *De Copia* (1512), an authoritative manual on composition, Erasmus stresses the need for copying and elaborating or varying the material. He illustrates this by giving 150 variations of the sentence "Your letter pleased me very much."[9]

The author distinguishes three stages in language learning, each divided into three parts—natural acquisition, generalization or systematic grammar, and practice, in which the student applies the rules already learned by extending them to new situations.

Stage I is accomplished at home or if possible in the nursery. The first steps are taken by naming, conversation, and description.

Stage II corresponds to the earliest school years, about the age of seven. Previous learning forms a basis for enlarging the student's powers of conversation. This is the time for simple readings such as those in the easier *Colloquies*. Pictures are used; for example, a garden is laid out with shaded walks and terraces containing all kinds of fruits and common plants. From this the student learns vocabulary directly from the object, not by the translation. Systematic grammar is still limited. Erasmus continues to stress that grammar follows speech: "It is by conversation and reading that the student learns a language, not by learning grammar."[10] He stresses the need to provide examples for any rules and to have the foreign language, Latin, as close as possible to everyday life.

Stage III requires a more thorough mastery of grammar. Practice is extended from the previous stage, but more reading is done. The purpose of reading is threefold: verifying and amplifying grammar rules (accidence, syntax, and prosody are illustrated and practiced), expanding vocabulary, and developing style.

In this way, progress in language learning moves from practice, in which the eye and ear become accustomed to words and sentences, to generalization—rules and paradigms are deduced from usage—to application of rules to extended practice in reading and conversation.

The author's approach to language teaching is best summarized in a passage from *De Ratione Studii (Upon the Right Method of Instruction)* (Part 3, Section 521C–522A):

> Whilst a knowledge of the rules of accidence and syntax is most necessary to every student, still they should be as few, as simple, and as carefully framed as possible. I have no patience with the stupidity of the average teacher of grammar who wastes precious years in hammering rules into children's heads. For it is not by learning rules that we acquire the power of speaking a language, but by daily intercourse with those accustomed to expressing themselves with exactness and refinement, and by the copious reading of the best authors.[11]

From Erasmus' work come four points that are today cornerstones of modern language teaching: (1) rules of usage are derived from an examination of the language; (2) grammar rules should be presented only after the grammar pattern has been learned in context, in a reading passage, or by other means; (3) grammar rules should always be accompanied by examples; and (4) where possible, pictures should be used to illustrate new material.

Another leading educator of the period was John Palsgrave. Born in London in 1480 of a good family, Palsgrave studied logic and philosophy at Cambridge. Further studies in Paris provided the opportunity to gain excellent command of French, and in 1514 he was appointed to teach French to a daughter of Henry VIII.[12] Palsgrave was the first to reduce French grammar to rules and illustrate them by examples. The results of his studies were published in 1530 in a volume titled *L'éclaircissement de la langue française.* The study included one book on pronunciation, another on grammar per se, including a section of lexical comparisons, and a third book of observations and commentaries on book two.

In contrasting French and English, Palsgrave distinguishes a difference in pronunciation and phrasing of the two languages. He notices that the French are "brefe and sodayne in soundyng of theyr wordes" and that they "gyve every word that they abyde and reste upon, theyr most audible sounde." Regarding stress, Palsgrave states, "The frenche men judgyng a worde to be most parfaytly herde, whan his last end is sounded hyghest, use generally to gyve theyr accent upon the last syllable onely."[13] But he also cites a condition under which stress falls on the penultimate syllable, explaining that one-syllable words receive no stress and that there is no pause between them within a sentence:

And that is one great cause why theyr tong seemeth to use so brefe and sodayn and so harde to be understanded whan it is spoken; for, thoughe there come never so many wordes of one syllable together, they pronounce them nat distinctly . . . but sounde them all under one voyce and tenor, except the commyng next unto a poynt be the cause there of. . . .[14]

The author observes that considerable difference exists between spoken and written French, and he employs a phonetic alphabet to illustrate certain features of pronunciation.[15] Following is a graphic and phonetic representation:

> loingtain imitateur des orateurs, salut
> [lointaynymitatevrdesoratevrsalevt]*

The section on lexicon contains the word alone, with its definition, and in a sentence in both languages, as follows:

> I ADVENTURE, I put in hazard or daunger.
> Je aduenture, prim. conj. If an man wyll
> accompany me, I dare adventure it: sy ame
> me veut accompaigner, je lose aduenturer.[16]

Especially for language-teaching purposes, Palsgrave's analysis is probably the most astute comparison of two languages done to that date and is one of the earliest successful attempts at contrastive analysis.

After Erasmus, the most important language scholar of the middle centuries was John Amos Comenius (1592–1670), the Czech theologian and educator who wrote several treatises on language teaching. In his earliest work, the *Janua Lingua (The Gates of Language Unlocked)* (1631), the author states that the first exercises in a new tongue should deal with subject matter students already know. In this way the learner advances from few things to the many, from brief material to the more lengthy, from the simple to the more complex, and from the regular to the irregular.[17]

Since there are many words beyond the capacity of the

* Following current linguistic practice, I will use < > to indicate material written alphabetically, [ ] for phonetic material, and / / for phonemic notations.

young scholar, Comenius recommends a controlled vocabulary. Moreover, the custom of the times in teaching vocabulary was to present only one meaning of a word. Comenius urges that several usual meanings of a word be taught. The *Janua Lingua* contains one hundred chapters with a thousand Latin sentences and their vernacular equivalents arranged in parallel columns. It also includes a chosen vocabulary of eight thousand words. The sentences, at first simple, gradually become more and more complex. Words are arranged so as to bring out concords, governments, and declensions. The subject matter includes such things as fire, stone, metal, trees, animals, man, mechanical arts, the house and its parts, the family, and the state. In treating the material, each chapter should be read ten times: (1) in the first reading, the material is translated into the vernacular; (2) in the second, the whole piece is written out, in Latin and in the vernacular; (3) the teacher reads the Latin aloud, and the students translate into the vernacular without looking at the page; (4) special attention is given to word derivations; (5) special attention is given to inflections; (6) the teacher explains synonyms; (7) the teacher illustrates the application of grammar rules; (8) students learn the text by heart; (9) the students perform a logical analysis of the subject matter; and (10) reading is conducted by the pupils, who challenge one another to repeat portions of the text.[18]

The *Janua Lingua* embodies one of Comenius' basic rules of language teaching: that words and things should never be divorced, that knowledge of the thing explained should be presented at the same time as the language itself.

This principle was further developed in the *Orbis Pictus*, published in 1657 and written on a plan similar to the *Janua*

Lingua. The new volume covered a wide range of topics but offered as a new methodology the extensive use of pictures. The following passage gives weight to the significance of visual aids, which were one of Comenius' specific contributions to foreign language teaching.

> ... if the objects are not present, the senses grow dull and flit hither and thither out of weariness. But when the objects are present, they [the students] grow merry, wax lively and willingly suffer themselves to be fastened upon them till the things be sufficiently discerned.[19]

The picture appears on one page and the text facing it on the other. Everything mentioned in the text is numbered in the picture and is in Latin as well as the vernacular:

Schola (1)	A school (1)
est officina in qua novelli	is a shop in which young wits
animi formantur ad virtutem	are fashioned to virtue
et distinguitur in classes.	and it is distinguished into classes.
Praeceptor (2)	The master (2)
sedet in cathedra (3)	sits in a chair (3)
discipuli (4)	the scholars (4)
in subsellus. (5)	in forms. (5)
Ille docet, hi discunt.	He teaches, they learn.
Quidam sedent	Some (students) sit
ad mensam et scribunt. (6)	at a table and write. (6)
Ipse corrigit mendas. (7)	He mendeth their faults. (7)[20]

Number 6 in the above refers to a woodcut depicting several students sitting at a table writing.

Comenius continued the tradition begun by Quintilian. Instead of learning rules, one learns by hearing and reading, by written and oral imitation, and by conversation.[21] He criticizes the custom of teaching the rules of the foreign language, Latin, in Latin: "The unknown is taught by the equally unknown."[22] This fault can be remedied if the teacher speaks the same vernacular as the students, and examinations are given in the vernacular. Above all, there must be frequent repetition and exercise in everything.

Most of Charles Hoole's professional experience was as a headmaster of a Yorkshire grammar school and principal of a private school in London. His *New Discovery of the Old Art of Teaching Schoole* was a companion piece to the treatises of Comenius. It was Hoole who translated the *Orbis Pictus* into English about two years before the publication of his own volume, which came out in 1660. Hoole put into practice many of Comenius' theories on language teaching. He states, "There is nothing in understanding that does not come through the senses," and criticizes the practice of appealing neither to the senses nor to understanding but to "sheer unreasoned memory." Partly because of his encouragement, visual aids became a more and more prominent part of foreign language teaching.

In the 1600's the vernacular began to reassert itself. By the middle of the century, priority was given to the mother tongue over all other languages including Latin. The reasons for this were several: the rise and unification of vernacular languages; the success of Protestantism, which used the vernaculars and helped them supplant Latin as the medium of instruction in non-Catholic universities; the loss of economic and practical value of Latin in a newly emerging commercial society; and the corresponding demand for courses that had such value.[23]

As Latin gradually lost its usefulness, Latin teachers began to justify its presence more and more as a mental discipline and source of cultural values. The original goals of oral fluency gave way to dissection, analysis, and parsing of several hundred lines each semester. A change in objectives brought with it a change in language-teaching methodology. Immediately after learning the rudiments, students were plunged into the classical writers such as Caesar and Cicero, with their complex sentence structure. The practice of establishing automatic recall by repetition and overlearning was completely eliminated. By the end of the seventeenth century, the concept of translation into the vernacular had completely supplanted the oral method.[24] Thus was laid the foundation for the grammar-translation method, which is still followed by some of the more traditional exponents of language teaching.

Claude Marcel was the first to make a clear distinction between the four language skills: understanding (hearing), speaking, reading, and writing. As separate activities, they should be learned independently. Possession of one skill does not confer mastery of another, for skills are manifested by different sense organs and meet different social purposes. "The same words a person reads easily fail to be recognized when they fall from the lips." And as if to drive home the point: "Reading a thousand books does not enable a person to understand a single word of the spoken language."[25]

Marcel regroups the four language skills into several binary systems:

1a. Understanding and speaking comprise the spoken language.
 b. Reading and writing comprise the written language.

2a. In reading and hearing, words recall the ideas.

    b. In speaking and writing, ideas suggest the words.

3a. Curiosity is the source of progress in reading and hearing.
   b. Imitation is the source of progress in speaking and writing.[26]

Each skill is made habitual by practice, leaving the mind free to concentrate on the next one. A previously learned skill may contribute to mastery of the next one. Comprehension is necessary before a person can produce language. "It is only after ideas have been conveyed to our minds by means of signs, that we can, by imitation, use these very signs to express the same or similar ideas."[27] In order to develop understanding and mastery of the passive skills, the author urges that teaching begin with reading and hearing, which he calls impression, as opposed to speaking and writing, or expression. The child is impelled to listen long before he can speak and owes his foundation to example, not to precepts. The ability to understand the written and spoken language leads to the arts of speaking and writing.

Marcel suggests that in developing reading skill, we cannot prepare by learning grammar or vocabulary in isolation, for in learning, the perception of an object always precedes consideration of its parts. We gain a knowledge of words by frequent exposure to them in specific contexts. In a scheme reminiscent of Fries's system of form classes, the author divides words into two groups: words significant in themselves —substantives, verbs, adjectives—and words serving to connect and complete the sense of the other group—articles, prepositions, conjunctions. Though of secondary importance, words in the second group "are the binding links of discourse, and materially modify the sense of the sentence."[28] For this reason acquaintance with them is useful if gained at the beginning or in conjunction with reading practice.

In order of importance, hearing is the first skill, as becomes readily apparent to a person who finds himself in the country of the target language. With the ability to understand (hear), a person can retain phrases and increase his powers more easily than with a knowledge of any other single skill.

Marcel is one of the first to employ the principle of substitution frames for developing competence in speaking. The first sentence must be simple and contain only known items. The teacher should then substitute "other words of the same species."[29] After that, the student will practice making variations on the text, modifying the sentence in a hundred ways before he parts with it. "Half the knowledge with twice the power of applying it, is better than twice the knowledge with half the power of application."[30]

The first Latin grammar in Anglo-Saxon was written by Aelfric, Abbot of Eynsham, around the year 1000. It was composed for school children and employed the eight parts of speech and other categories used in Latin. In his preface the author states that the book will serve as an introduction to English (Anglo-Saxon) grammar. He assumed that the ancient grammatical framework of Greek and Latin would work for another language, the first time such a method was formally suggested.[31]

In 1513, William Lily, with the aid of Erasmus, published the first Latin grammar in English. Lily's work is important for English grammar, since in it the Latin paradigm was put beside the English translation. Such an arrangement suggested that English forms be presented in the same way with the same terminology. In 1542, Henry VIII made it the standard text for school use.[32]

This attitude was carried further by Ben Jonson, whose book *The English Grammar* (1640), the most important seventeenth-century work on the subject, contains all of the linguistic baggage handed down from the ancients. By the time Jonson's grammar was published, courses in reading, writing, and spelling in English had already been added to the curriculum of elementary schools and some lower classes of grammar schools. The movement to institute such vernacular studies was led by Comenius and Hoole.

Unfortunately, most eighteenth-century grammarians followed the precedent of Jonson and other seventeenth-century writers in modeling their English texts on Latin grammars. There were exceptions such as William Loughton, a Kensington schoolmaster who strongly argued against forcing the language, "contrary to its nature, to the method and rule of the Latin grammar."[33] He even discarded the terms *noun*, *adjective*, and *verb*, in favor of *names*, *qualities*, and *affirmations*. But the view of most grammarians was that language had passed its golden age and had entered a period of decadence. Though interest in grammar increased greatly, especially during the last third of the century, attention shifted to philosophical speculation on the nature and origin of language, the possibilities of a universal grammar, and remodeling English into greater conformity with logic and order.[34] In the last half of the eighteenth century, men like Samuel Johnson, Joseph Priestly, and George Campbell reintroduced the doctrine of usage as the guide to correctness.

Samuel Johnson's dictionary was published in 1755 after seven years of preparation. Though marred by many ludicrous etymologies and other faults, it soon became the recognized standard. Two elements in particular have significance for language analysis and language teaching. First, by separating and numbering word meanings, he treated the English vocabulary more fully than it had ever been done before. For example, he defines *man* in the following way:

1. A human being
2. Not a woman
3. Not a boy
4. A servant; an attendant; a dependent
5. A word of familiarity bordering on contempt
6. It is used in loose signification like the French *on*, one, any one[35]

Second, and even more important, was the citing of contexts to show particular meaning or usage. From his wide reading Johnson copied down sentences and passages in which a particular word occurred. He later used these excerpts to illustrate meanings.

In the *Plan* of his dictionary, Johnson states:

> It is not in our power to have recourse to any established laws of speech; but we must remark how the writers of former ages have used the same word. . . . I shall therefore, since the rules of stile, like those of law, arise from precedents often repeated, collect the testimonies on both sides, and endeavor to promulgate the decrees of custom, who has so long possessed . . . the sovereignty of word.[36]

Though Johnson followed the traditionalists in his use of grammatical terms, the language teaching aspects of his lexical studies are significant. Johnson's dictionary "was long the dominant model for men who hoped to shape the language, to record its changes, or to prevent them."[37]

More typical of eighteenth-century attitudes was Robert Lowth's *Short Introduction to English Grammar* (1762). To Lowth, the main purpose of grammar is "to teach us to express ourselves with propriety in that language. . . . The plain way of doing this is to lay down rules and illustrate them by example."[38] He drew "right" and "wrong" examples from such writers as Shakespeare, Pope, Addison, and Dryden, maintaining that the English language, "as it is spoken by the politest part of the nation, and as it stands in the writing of the most approved authors, often offends against every part of grammar."[39] Lowth's text was used at Harvard between 1774 and 1841 and had its effect on later American grammarians.[40]

Over and against Lowth were a few men like Joseph Priestly, lonely echoes from the eighteenth century who championed usage as the basis of linguistic analysis. As a young man, Priestly showed great ability in Oriental languages and from them may have discovered the impossibility of trying to describe one language with the grammatical system of another.

In his two treatises, *Theory of Language* (1762) and especially *The Rudiments of English Grammar* (1761), he tried to record what he had observed rather than succumbing to preconceptions of right and wrong:

> I am surprised to see so much of the . . . technical terms of Latin grammar retained in the grammar of our own tongue, where they are exceedingly awkward and absolutely superfluous; being such as could not possibly have entered into the

head of any man, who had not been previously acquainted with Latin.[41]

> It seems wrong to confound the account of inflections either with the grammatical uses of the combinations of words in the order in which they are placed, or of the words which express relations and which are equivalent to inflections in other languages.[42]

His revolt against Latin grammar was based on the belief that "the custom of speaking is the original and only just standard of any language."[43]

Some of his linguistic insights are extremely perceptive:

> A little reflection may . . . suffice to convince any person that we have no more business with a future tense in our own language than we have with the whole system of Latin moods and tenses, because we have no modification of our verbs to correspond to it. . . . It should be no more given a particular name with the auxiliaries *shall* and *will*, than those that are made with the auxiliaries *do, have, can, must*, or any other.[44]

This same concept has been applied in such modern EFL texts as *English Sentence Patterns* by Robert Lado and Charles Fries, which includes the auxiliaries *can, could, will, may, might*, and *must* in the same pattern and presents them all in the same chapter.

Priestly insisted that the grammar of a language would never be affected by the arbitrary rules of men:

> A language can never be properly fixed, till all the varieties with which it is used, have been held forth to public view, and the general preference of certain forms declared, by the general practice afterwards. . . . It must be allowed that the custom of speaking is the original and only standard of any language.[45]

In *The Rudiments of English Grammar,* he follows the best and most numerous authorities, urging the use of modern rather than early writers. If they are contradictory, he resorts to analogy. "If this should decide for neither of two contrary practices, the thing must remain undecided, till all-governing custom shall declare in favor of one or the other."[46]

More important than Priestly in promoting the doctrine of usage was George Campbell, whose *Philosophy of Rhetoric* appeared in 1776. Somewhat caustically he states:

> It is not the business of grammar, as some critics seem preposterously to imagine, to give law to the fashions which regulate speech. On the contrary, from its conformity to these [fashions of speech], and from that alone, it derives all its authority and value.[47]

He further elaborates that the grammar of any language is nothing but a collection of general observations methodically digested, by which all significations, derivations, and combinations of words in that language are ascertained.

As a step beyond Priestly, Campbell describes what constitutes this authoritative body of usage. It includes present, national, and reputable use. *Reputable* is defined as "whatever modes of speech are authorized as good by the writing of a great number, if not the majority of celebrated authors."[48]

After the American Revolution, the rise of English grammar became extremely rapid as Latin declined. Grammar was regarded as the art of speaking and writing, acquired by page after page of rote memorizing. Grammar study was begun by very young children and was accompanied by no oral discussion of composition. In short, it proceeded on the wrong basis —inflections—and began with the wrong unit—the word—

and with the wrong methods, going from theory and rules to practice. Texts were modeled after Latin grammars, and authors advised methods that had been used in the teaching of Latin for three hundred years. Throughout the early and middle years of the nineteenth century, American grammarians tended to favor the more conservative interpretations of people like Lowth, and there is little to learn from them in language teaching or language analysis.

Toward the 1850's a school of language teaching appeared that focused on the sentence as the unit of meaning. The new approach was championed by such men as Roswell Smith and Samuel Greene. Greene's work is probably the most remarkable analysis of the English language up to the advent of the structural linguists in the 1920's. Many of his pedagogical principles are extremely sound and have definite application to foreign-language teaching. And certain of his lessons give the impression of being designed more for foreign students than for native speakers. For these reasons, an analysis of his work may provide some interesting footnotes in the history of language teaching theory.

Greene stresses doing as more important to the learning process than memorization of grammar rules: "Children perceive grammatical . . . relations more easily from what they have to perform, than from what they have to commit to memory."[49] An initial volume, *First Lessons in Grammar based on the Construction and Analysis of Sentences*, is divided into two parts: "The Formation of Words, Orthography and Etymology" and "The Formation of Sentences." "The principal feature of the work consists in unfolding the principles of grammar in connection with the construction and analysis of sentences. . . . The sentence is brought, at first, in its simplest state. The learner is next made to witness its growth by the addition of words, phrases and clauses."[50]

Greene states that every sentence has meaning and form and that form may change while meaning remains constant. He urges the study of form as well as meaning in a sentence: "The form of a sentence changes when its *elements* change":

> An *industrious* man will gain a competence.
> A man of *industry* will gain a competence.
> A man who is *industrious* will gain a competence.[51]

He states that there is no difference in the meaning of these sentences.

> The facilities which are thus afforded for an interchange of equivalent *words, phrases,* or *clauses* . . . have been too much overlooked in treatises on the English language. As soon, then, as the pupil becomes familiar with the distinctive features of these three classes of the elements, he should have frequent examination on equivalents.[52]

Greene's definition of grammar as the formation of words and the formation of sentences corresponds to our current components of morphology and syntax. In the introduction to *First Lessons* he discusses the building of a sentence. The explication runs something like this:

1a. A statement may consist of two words: *Horses ran.* However, it tells us nothing about horses, for example, how many horses ran.
 b. Two horses ran.

2a. This is far too general. We would ask: What kind of horses ran?
 b. Two white horses ran.

3a. In what condition were they?
 b. Two white horses which were attached to a coach ran.

4a. How did they run?
 b. Two white horses which were attached to a coach ran furiously.

5a. Where?
 b. Two white horses which were attached to a coach ran furiously through the streets of Boston.

6a. When?
 b. Two white horses which were attached to a coach ran furiously through the streets of Boston one morning in June.

7a. Why?
 b. Two white horses which were attached to a coach ran furiously through the streets of Boston one morning in June, because they were frightened by falling timbers.[53]

Additions may be single words, as in *b* of sentences 1, 2, and 4, or groups of words, as in sentences 3, 5, 6, 7, and 8, and the parts of a sentence may be either words or groups of words. A sentence must consist of two essential parts only, like 1b or 2b, or it must contain those two parts with additions.

Greene makes some useful comments and suggestions. For example, he observes that the English language contains forty sounds.* These sounds are divided into vocals (vowels), sub-vocals (voiced consonants), and aspirates (voiceless consonants). Many letters have two or more distinct sounds (name, far, war, what), while the same sound is often represented by different letters, for example: /z/ amaze, was.

* According to some authorities, American English contains thirty-three segmental phonemes.[54]

Greene classifies words by their formation and distinguishes a primitive or radical word (a word in no way derived from another, for example, *form, harm*); a derivative word (a word formed by joining to a primitive some letter or syllable to modify its meaning, for example, *reform, harmless*); a compound word (a word formed by uniting two or more entire words, for example, *inkstand, schoolhouse*). These concepts are taught by practice. The author directs: "From derivative words form the following primitives . . . hope, fear, harm, love, care, know . . . cloud, joy, truth, poet . . . ."[55] He also treats the other two groups in the same manner.

In a section on prefixes, Greene points out the operation of assimilation: "The final letter of a prefix is often changed to one which will harmonize, in sound, with the initial letter of a radical, as: *impious*, for *in-pious*. The final letter of the prefix generally becomes the same as the first letter of the radical: *il-limitable*."[56] As an assignment, he gives a prefix followed by certain words, and the student is to combine the prefix with the words (words which cause assimilation to occur). He also presents a list of prefixes of Latin, Greek, and what he calls Saxon origin:

Prefix	Signification	Example
mis	wrong, error	mistake, misspell
over	above, beyond	overdo, overload
un	not, negation	unwise, unkind

Then he develops the concept of affixing in the following way: "Study the list of prefixes, then add to the following roots all that may be used appropriately: cede (to go, to yield), clude (to shut, or close), fuse, press, pel (to urge or drive). . . . By exercises like the above, multiplied at the discretion of the teacher, the pupil may soon perceive the force of all the prefixes."[57] Greene also offers a similar presentation of suffixes.

In Part II, "The Formation of Sentences," he discusses attributes (adjectives) and gives two positions for them: assumed (blue sky, rough sea, poisonous reptile) and predicated (the sea is rough; the sky is blue). For practice, he has the student assume porous, rough, and yellow as qualities of gold and pure, clear, salt, and fresh as qualities of water, then predicate the same qualities. He also instructs the student to assume and predicate the action of bees, whales, waves, merchants, and others. Model: *buzzing* bees (assumed) and bees *buzz* or *are buzzing* (predicated).

Greene's analysis and pedagogy, nearly a century before the publications of the English Language Institute, University of Michigan, provide a definite basis for the structural pattern drill. He further offers a number of substitution drills for subject, verb, and object positions as well as for subject-verb number agreement; modals; and conversions, for example, statement>question.

In presenting phrase modifiers of predicates, Greene distinguishes objective (They began to sing) and adverbial modifiers (We left on Tuesday). Then for objective, students "write infinitives as objects to complete the meaning of the following predicates: *We wish, They know how, We did not intend to, The boys hope,*" and others. For adverbial modifiers, students write sentences of their own, "limiting the predicates by the following phrases: over the hill, on the ground, up the tree, to New York, from Philadelphia, toward the East, around the garden."[58] Model: The horses ran *over the hill*. Also included is a section of "miscellaneous" forms that fit into the pattern, such as *ten miles* in *He ran ten miles*. Modification is also taught by adjective or participle at the beginning of a sentence. Students are given a list of words to use—*eager, anxious, encircled, regardless, aware, ambitious,* and others—along with a model: *Eager to attain the highest rank,* he labored incessantly. Finally, they have to produce sentences using the given words and following the model.

A second volume, published several years later,[59] includes a perceptive analysis of the "double object" pattern, in which the author places three attributes in the second object position:

	an officer	(substantive attribute)
They made the man	jealous	(adjective attribute)
	labor	(verbal attribute)

Sometimes a participle is used in the second object position, as in *I hear him speaking.* Greene points out that verbs which fit the pattern include *make, appoint, elect, create, constitute, render, name, style, call, esteem, think, consider, regard, reckon,* and others.

It is difficult to know to what extent ideas are influenced by those of previous generations. We do know that Greene's texts enjoyed wide success, and it is possible that many EFL practices before and after 1940 made their way, directly or indirectly, from Greene's little volumes.

The next positive step in language teaching was a system known as the natural method, developed by Gottlieb Heness in 1866 in his small school in New Haven. It is essentially a series of monologues by the teacher, interspersed with an exchange of questions and answers between teacher and pupils. Only the target language is used in class, with gestures, pictures, and objects in the immediate environment providing the subject matter.

Heness was later joined by Lambert Sauveur, who became the chief exponent of the system. Although its value was highly controversial, many textbook writers were strongly influenced by Heness and Sauveur, especially their insistence on conversational practice.[60] Sauveur explains the method in his book, *Introduction to the Teaching of Living Languages without Grammar or Dictionary*. Throughout the first year, "not a word of English is pronounced, and everything is understood."[61] The teachers start with realia—fingers, hands, parts of the body—gradually introducing objects in class and later principal tenses by means of time words like *yesterday, today* and *tomorrow*. Sauveur explains:

> I raise my finger before you, and show it to you. Do you not understand, whatever your language may be, that that means *there is the finger?* ... Then I count my ten fingers and you count with me, always in French, the target language. ... I turn my forefinger to myself, pronouncing these words, *I have ten fingers*; and I add instantly, pointing my finger towards you, *You have ten fingers, madame.* Immediately I commence to make you speak, by asking you how many fingers you have. ... To a second question, *How many fingers have I?* You answer me, *You have ten fingers.*[62]

Here is the author's methodology and procedure for a sample lesson. At home students read a selection on how Montaigne was taught Latin. Once in class the pupils keep their books closed, for "the ear alone must be occupied there."[63] The teacher gives a sentence and the student responds in the following way:

TCHR: Montaigne is in advance; we are in the background [of language learning].
STUD : How did he learn Latin?

Tchr: Listen, he began when he was quite young.
Stud : Who was his teacher?
Tchr: A German.
Stud : Did he [the teacher] speak French well?
Tchr: Fortunately not; he did not know a word of it.
Stud : What did he do?
Tchr: He [the teacher] spoke Latin.
Stud : Did he explain the lessons to the little boy?
Tchr: Impossible, since he did not have French at his command.
Stud : Had he a grammar?
Tchr: Neither grammar nor dictionary, Montaigne tells us in Chapter XXV of the "Essays."
Stud : What did the little boy do?
Tchr: He did just as you are doing. He listened to his teacher; he answered his teacher; and like you, he was curious and asked questions.[64]

Initially, the teacher imparts grammar much as the parent teaches the child—by ear, not by eye, always speaking and never using a single English word in school. For this reason, grammar is not taught in the beginning but at the end, when pupils are familiar with the spoken method. Grammar is introduced after the first year, the students by this time acquainted with grammatical forms before actually studying them. The only remaining need is to examine the most complicated points, those that are even difficult for native speakers.

Turning to vocabulary, Sauveur declares, "The means of learning the words of a language is not to think about them but to produce ideas constantly, using for instruments only the words of the language one is studying."[65] In other words, the student's vocabulary should be surrogate to thought content, so that other mental faculties besides memory will be stimulated and ease in using the language gained by exciting interest in the exchange of ideas. Composition consists only of the phrases that have been acquired orally.

≈ III ≈

The Development of Linguistic and Language Teaching Theory in the United States, 1880-1940

FROM 1870 TO 1925 linguistic science was concerned chiefly with the comparison of Indo-European languages, or comparative linguistics, and the reconstruction of European, or historical, linguistics. A result of such investigations was increasing interest in the phenomenon of sound change, supplemented with new insights into the processes of analogical creation and borrowing. This concern for sound changes and the importance of sounds provided considerable impetus in the development of phonetics. Before 1940 the main contribution of linguistics to language teaching was in the area of phonology (phonetics and phonemics). "Before 1940, American descriptive linguistics had very little to contribute to the analysis or statement of syntax."[1]

For this reason, any study of linguistic theory from 1880 to 1940 must center on phonology, the men involved in its development, and its applications to language teaching. This chapter will also examine some of the indigenous American work in anthropological linguistics and the structural concepts that emerged from them in morphology and syntax.

The invention of a special phonetic alphabet in English

33

goes back at least to the work of John Hart, who in 1570 used his own system for teaching reading and spelling improvement.[2] Hart was probably the first English writer to deal with phonetic problems in a systematic way. Several concepts important for language teaching have emerged from his work. First, he distinguished the relationship between voiced and voiceless sounds, for example, [b-p], [d-t].[3] Second, he recognized the organic positions of speech sounds, differentiating between stops and continuants. Third, he explained the function of sounds in running speech. He warned against giving names to letters in isolation (Aee, Bee), and recommended teaching the sounds themselves. According to Hart, letters, or alphabets, were originally an attempt to reproduce man's voice graphically:

> The inventors of letters, whatsoever they were, had a regard to mans voice: considering how mani diverse simple wais, he mought use his toung, and lippes with his voice in his speech. . . . This being true, I may boldli say, that even as the voices in speaking do make a word, so the letters which ar their markes, and figures shall do the like in writing: seing that voices ar as elements, and the letters are their markes.[4]

Hart further suggests that since letters are the "images of mannes voice, ye ar forced to graunt that the writing shuld have so mani letters as the pronunciation neadeth of voices, and no more, or lesse: so that yf yt be found otherwise . . . yt is utterly to be refused." He cites the authority of Quintilian, stating that the old orator

"would have ðə raytiŋ freymd to ðə maner əv spiykiŋ."[5]

As a result of the relatively unphonetic nature of English spelling, one-quarter to one-third of the printed letters now

used are superfluous. In Hart's system there are "as many
letters in our writing, as we do voyces or breathes in speaking,
and no more: and neur to abuse one for another, and to
write as we speake."[6] Perhaps the most basic distinction in
Hart's system is the contrast between voiced and voiceless
sounds, with separate symbols for

/dʒ/ and /tʃ/, /ð/ and /þ/, and /ʃ/.
He further recognizes the pairing of /f/ and /v/, /t/ and
/d/, /p/ and /b/, /s/ and /z/, and /k/ and /g/.

Hart describes the voiced quality as "an inwarde sound, as
it were groning, ending with the breath thrust forth," and
the voiceless quality as "no sounde, but the breath onely."[7]

To help the students learn sound contrasts, he presents a
table with each box containing one of seven minimal pairs,
juggling the order of presentation in following rows to give
students practice in producing the sounds quickly. It is not
difficult to see in such a system the concept of minimal pairs,
later used in EFL teaching.[8]

bp	dt	gk	dʒtʃ	vf	ðþ	zs
vf	ðþ	zs	bp	dt	gk	dʒtʃ
gk	dʒtʃ	vf	ðþ	zs	bp	dt
zs	bp	dt	gk	dʒtʃ	vf	ðþ
ðþ	zs	bp	dt	gk	dʒtʃ	vf
dt	gk	dʒtʃ	vf	ðþ	zs	bp
dʒtʃ	vf	ðþ	zs	bp	dt	gk

Many others as well experimented with phonetic alphabets and the analysis of speech sounds. John Wilkins (1614–72), for example, employed the concept of opposition in analyzing and classifying sounds. Anticipating the phonemic principle, he states that letters do not represent shades of sounds but the "principal heads of them."[9] These principal heads, suggests Albright, are comparable to the "distinctive units in phonemics."[10] Applied to vowels, Wilkins' phonemic analysis produced eight distinct vowel sounds, plus possible intermediate sounds which, "by reason of their proximity to those others, prove so difficult of distinction, as would render them useless."[11]

But the most striking progress in phonology did not come until the nineteenth century. Pursuing the development of a phonetic alphabet, Isaac Pitman and A. J. Ellis tried to introduce a system that would replace an inconsistent and confused spelling with one that would help destroy prevailing illiteracy and promote the reading and spelling ability of children, illiterate adults, and foreigners. Pitman and Ellis followed the principle that a sound should always be represented by the same symbol, "although individual symbols might have different meanings attached to them in different situations."[12] From 1850 to 1876, Pitman, working without Ellis, developed an alphabet which was the first one used by the International Phonetic Association in 1886.

Another designer of phonetic alphabets was Alexander M. Bell, whose purpose was similar to that of John Hart: to make reading easier for children and foreigners and to aid in the pronunciation of native and foreign languages.[13] Bell's most important contribution to phonetics was his system of terminology, especially his front-back, high-low system of classifying vowels. His arrangement presented two constantly intersecting movements of tongue positions—high-mid-low and front-mixed-back—the only difference today being the substitution of *central* for *mixed*. Minor degrees of difference from these primary vowels were indicated by diacritic marks. In investigating the nature of consonant sounds, Bell perceived a new class of elements, intermediate between vowels and consonants. These he called glides or semi-vowels, which "completed the scheme of linguistic sounds, joining the vowels and consonants into one harmonious scale."[14]

Bell's new system was quite different from other known alphabets:

> Each organ and each mode of organic action concerned in the production or modification of sound, has its appropriate symbol; and all sounds of the same nature produced at different parts of the mouth, are represented by a single symbol turned in a direction corresponding to the organic position.[15]

Although the author's alphabet is very strange to look at, "his system is the first which gives a really adequate and comprehensive view of the whole field of possible sounds," suggests Henry Sweet. "Bell did more for phonetics than all his predecessors put together."[16]

One of the high points in the history of phonetics was the creation of the International Phonetic Association in 1886. Designed to be international and applicable to all languages, the International Phonetic Alphabet (IPA) had twenty-six vowels and fifty-two consonant sounds at the time of its founding in 1888.

Begun originally by language teachers, the association was

at first more interested in pedagogy than in phonetics and focused initially on improving the teaching of foreign languages. Among the principles it recommended were:

1. One must study the spoken language rather than the archaic language.
2. The first aim in language teaching is to make the student completely familiar with the sounds of the foreign language.
3. The instructor should teach the most usual *phrases* and idiomatic expressions, by means of: continuous texts, dialogues, descriptions and narration.
4. Grammar should be taught inductively as a corollary to and generalization of the facts observed during reading.
5. Expressions in the target language should relate directly to ideas or other expressions in the target language, not to those of the maternal language, thus as far as possible, replacing translation by direct associations with the target language.[17]

By the middle of the 1920's the most advanced phoneticians were coming to realize that the description of a sound system must be a concept rather than a physical entity, since the existence of twelve *p*'s and twenty *t*'s, for example, would make language teaching or analysis extremely unwieldy.[18] The solution to this problem lay in the concept of the phoneme, which emerged toward the end of the nineteenth century.

It was the Polish philologist Jan Baudouin de Courtenay (1845–1929) who first used the word *phoneme* in its modern sense.[19] Although he probably worked out the phoneme principle during the 1870's,[20] his theories remained unnoticed by European linguists for a long time, perhaps because of the poor contact between Western scholars and Russia, where he taught. His work reached western Europe, especially England, through many of his students, a German translation of his studies appearing in 1895. "It is only in the last 15 years," stated Trubetzkoy in 1933, "that the idea of a fundamental distinction between sounds and phonemes has begun to be circulated in the world."[21]

But ideas have no allegiance to their creators, and it seems that other linguists began arriving at similar conclusions independently. In England as early as 1870, Henry Sweet made the distinction between significant and non-significant elements. Though he did not use the term *phoneme*, "his realization of the principle was shown by the distinction he drew between 'broad' and 'narrow' types of phonetic transcription."[22]

On the Continent, the concept was strengthened by the work of the Geneva school led by Ferdinand de Saussure.[23] "We speak of a phoneme," says de Saussure, "as one would speak of a zoological species; there are male and female examples, but no ideal examples of the species."[24] Actually, de Saussure never sufficiently established the conditions under which two sounds are included in the same phoneme.[25] But his distinction of *langue* and *parole* did provide a foundation. *Langue* is an abstract linguistic system existing quite apart from the individual. It is not spoken by anybody, but is a composite reflecting different dialects. *Parole,* on the other hand, is the physical reality that varies from person to person, and may include different dialects of native speakers. This contrast provided the basis for later work in dialect geography, and *langue,* of course, gave conceptual form to the phoneme.

In his attitude toward language, de Saussure embodied a

mentalist view, that human language cannot be studied as mere physical or animal conditioning. Human behavior is voluntary and as such involves analogy and the ability to reason from accumulated facts and ideas. Language teaching methods based on such a point of view tend to stress the importance of meanings in addition to physical forms.[26]

Another linguist responsible for the development of the phoneme was Nicholai Trubetzkoy (1890–1938), who, according to Gleason, wrote the first great work in European descriptive linguistics.[27] Influenced by de Saussure, Trubetzkoy was closely associated with Roman Jackobson and the Prague school of linguistics, whose chief contribution was its technique for determining the way a language structures its sound units into specific patterns. According to the Prague school, the criterion for determining which sounds are significantly contrastive is meaning. "Phonetic differences that do not signal semantic differences are not distinctive, are not phonemic."[28] In other words, the phoneme is not the sound itself but the sound's contrastive function. By around 1915 phonemic theory was being taught in the Department of Phonetics in the University of London.

In the United States it was Edward Sapir who, somewhat independently, recognized the role of the phoneme[29] and stimulated increasing interest and research with his article "Sound Patterns in Language." But American interest in phonemics became widespread after 1930, chiefly through the influence of Leonard Bloomfield. Thus by the time the concept of the phoneme was first given wide circulation, at the First International Congress of Linguists at The Hague in 1928, the ground had already been prepared.[30]

The phonemic cataloging of English took place largely between 1925 and 1950. In fact, during this period American linguistics was based almost wholly on the concept of the phoneme. Dissent did not become significant until the appearance of generative grammar in the late 1950's.[31]

One of the more peculiarly American fields of inquiry was that of anthropological linguistics, which more than anything else was responsible for the rise of structural linguistics and the applications of linguistics to foreign language teaching.

Far from a late-nineteenth-century phenomenon, interest in American Indian languages goes back to men like Peter Stephen DuPonceau (1760–1844), who came from France, fought in the Revolution, and stayed on to become a citizen. For his work in American Indian languages he received the French *Prix Volney* in 1838 for his "Mémoire sur le systeme grammatical des langues de quelques nations indiennes de l'Amérique du Nord."[32] It was DuPonceau who invented the term *polysynthetic*.

Others like John Pickering (1777–1846), secretary to the United States minister to Portugal, traveled widely, studying such languages as Arabic and Turkish. Returning to the United States, he became a specialist on the North American Indians, bringing with him an awareness of non-Indo-European patterns in the structure of language.

Another founder of Amerind linguistics was Samuel Haldeman, who became the recognized authority on the subject. The first professor of comparative philology in the University of Pennsylvania in 1856, he was a great admirer of the Sanskrit scholar William Jones. Haldeman devoted much time to English, Chinese, and other languages, being particularly interested in phonetics and alphabetic systems. His sense of hearing was said to be so acute that he could differentiate the sounds emitted by insects.[33]

But the field was really established by James Smithson (1765–1829) and the work of the Smithsonian Institution, which since 1850 has encouraged and sponsored research on American Indian and other "exotic" languages.[34] Much of the earliest work, done by missionaries, included such items as a grammar and lexicon of the Dakota Indians; a grammar and dictionary of Yoruba, West Africa; and a comparative phonology of four Sioux languages.

However, the man most closely associated with early Amerind studies is Franz Boas, the first professor of anthropology in Columbia University, 1899. It was Boas who developed techniques of descriptive linguistics as an integral part of anthropology, and his students later provided the impetus for the development of descriptive linguistics in the United States.[35] To Boas, "the unconsciously formed categories found in human speech have not been sufficiently exploited for the investigation of the categories into which the whole range of human experience is forced."[36]

Boas points out that the same grammatical categories do not appear in all languages. For example, certain apparently fundamental aspects of nouns in Indo-European languages— gender, singular and plural forms, syntactic combinations such as cases—are not necessary elements of articulate speech or of other language families. The Algonquin language divides nouns into animate and inanimate instead of masculine and feminine gender, and in Siouan the distinction between singular and plural is made with animate objects only.[37] Differences exist even in the distribution of personal pronouns.

For example, in Hottentot (South Africa), sex distinctions are made not only in the third person but also in the first and second. The same relativity obtains in syntactic categories. The English sentence "The man is sick" becomes in Eskimo "man sick," the concepts of time and place remaining indefinite. Each language, relative to other languages, may seem arbitrary in its classifications. "What appears as a single simple idea in one language may be characterized by a series of distinct phonetic groups in another."[38] How does this concept affect language learning?

> When we consider . . . what this implies, it will be recognized that in each language, only a part of the complete concept that we have in mind is expressed, and that each language has a peculiar tendency to select this or that aspect of the mental image which is conveyed by the expression of the thought.[39]

In situations where the students come from many language backgrounds, this awareness cannot really be utilized. But when all the students have a common native language, material can be designed to contrast phonological, grammatical, and semantic units of the two languages. This point will be examined more fully in Chapter VI.

In observing phonological systems, Boas points out that every language has a definite and limited number of sounds. Such a limited number is necessary for rapid communication. If the number were too large or unlimited, mechanical accuracy would be impossible, and understanding extremely difficult. A single sound has no independent existence by itself; it never enters into the consciousness of the speaker but exists only as a part of the sound complex that carries meaning. Boas defines the word as "a phonetic group which, owing to its permanence of form, clearness of significance, and phonetic independence, is readily separated from the whole sentence."[40] He stresses the sentence rather than the word as the natural unit of expression. However, his definition of the sentence as "a group of articulate sounds which convey a complete idea"[41] offers little help in understanding this most elusive syntactic unit.

For his insights and labors Boas may be considered the father of descriptive linguistics, and he was responsible for training and encouraging a whole school of disciples in the new science. His most notable pupil was Edward Sapir, who, together with Leonard Bloomfield, dominated the field and its course of development in the 1940's.

Work on American Indian languages caused a dramatic shift in emphasis from written sources, which were regarded as usually imprecise representations of the language, to a complete focus on speech.[42] From this new emphasis, Edward Sapir evolved his theory of descriptive linguistics based on the phoneme. The sound system thus became the starting point in language analysis. Sapir makes several observations, mostly in the areas of phonology and morphology, that have significance for language teaching.

He points out the importance of voiced over voiceless sounds, that voiced sounds carry most of the significant differences in pitch, stress, and syllabification.[43] He mentions four criteria that determine the proper position of any sound: the position of the vocal folds during articulation; whether the breath passes into the mouth alone or if it also enters the nose; whether the breath passes freely through the mouth or is impeded at some point and, if so, in what manner; and the precise points of articulation in the mouth.[44]

Comparing systems, one finds that different languages may distribute similar phonetic elements in different ways. For example, the sound /ts/ exists in both English and German, but it does not occur in word-initial position in English, except for the loan-word *tsetse* fly. Furthermore, some languages allow long strings of consonants, while in others no two consonants or vowels occur together. Even though two languages may theoretically have the same vowels and consonants, other factors can produce quite different acoustic effects. There may be difference in lengths or "qualities" of phonetic elements. One language may be sensitive to relative stress (English), while stress is a minor consideration in another (French). In certain languages such as English, pitch differences may not affect the word as such, while in others they may alter a meaning completely, as in Chinese and several African and Southeast Asian languages. An awareness of the various features is of great potential help in designing EFL material for students from a particular language background.

Phonemic considerations aside, it is really Sapir's morphemic analysis that determines his classification of language types. In analyzing different forms of additives (see below), he arrives at the following:

Analytic Language: One that either does not combine concepts into a single word, such as Chinese, or does so sparingly, such as English or French.

Synthetic Language: One in which "concepts cluster more thickly," but there is still a tendency to "keep the range of concrete significance in single words down to moderate compass."

Polysynthetic Language: One which is more than ordinarily synthetic. A much wider range of concepts is symbolized by affixes or change in the radical element. Syntactic relations may also be included. Subjacent to this scheme is Sapir's classification of word types,[45] quite like the system of Samuel Greene except for item four:

	Symbol	*Example*	*Description*
1.	A	sing	radical element alone
2.	A+(b)	singing, impossible	radical element, such as *sing* or *possible*, plus (b), a grammatical increment, or additive: an addition or change such as an affix, infix, reduplication, internal change, for example, song>sung, that places some formal limitation on the radical element and that virtually never appears alone but must be attached to a radical*
3.	A+B	houseboat	two or more independently occurring radical elements in a single term
4.	(A)+(B)	*hortus* (Latin: garden)	form in which the radical element does not exist as an independently intelligible or satisfying element in speech[46]

Linguists in the Sapir tradition began to search for grammatical concepts parallel to the phoneme and soon developed the idea of the morpheme, which enabled anthropological linguists to make great progress in the description of word formation. In a summary morphosyntactic statement, Sapir observes:

* In the notation song>sung, (>) will be used to indicate *becomes* or *changes to.*

46

Every language possesses one or more formal methods for indicating the relation of a secondary concept to the main concept of the radical element. Some of these grammatical processes, like suffixing, are exceedingly widespread; others, like vocalic change, are less common but far from rare; still others, like accent and consonant change, are somewhat exceptional as functional processes. Not all languages are as irregular as English in the assignment of functions to its stock of grammatical processes.[47]

An interesting study could be made of the different ways syntactic functions are combined into words. Such a study could be comparative, between two languages, or might focus on English itself. A good morphosyntactic analysis would have implications for the teaching of structure (grammar) as well as vocabulary.*

The most influential American linguist in the first half of the twentieth century was Leonard Bloomfield, who, more than any other individual, was responsible for making the study of language into a science. From Boas he derived the importance of "primitive" languages as a laboratory for testing the principles of investigation he later applied to English.[49] His article "Postulates for the Study of Language" established guidelines and offered rich suggestions for future language study.[50]

But his best-known work is *Language,* a revision of an earlier book surveying the field of linguistics.[51] Fries, writing in 1962, described it as "the most important single publication concerning the scientific study of language during the past

---

* The term *morphosyntactic* is merely suggestive. I have not come across it before. There exists the term *morphophonemics,* referring to phonemic change which results from combining morphemes.[48]

47

twenty-five years."[52] In reviewing the volume, Bernard Bloch states that "every significant refinement of analytic method produced in this country since 1930 has come as a direct result of the impetus given to linguistic research by Bloomfield's book.[53]

Actually, it was in his earlier volume (1914) that Bloomfield set out his principles of language teaching. Language learning consists of building up associative habits which constitute the language to be learned. American schools assume that reading rather than speaking is the aim of language teaching. But even here the desired associations cannot be formed without much oral and auditory practice.[54] The later volume defines his position, that "the thousands of morphemes and tagmemes of the foreign language, can be mastered only by constant repetition."[55]

> A student who does not know the sound of a language, finds great difficulty in learning to read it. He cannot remember the foreign forms so long as they figure for him as a mere jumble of letters. Aside from the esthetic factor, a clearcut set of phonetic habits . . . is essential to fluent and accurate reading.*

Instead of translation, work in the elementary stage should consist of repeated use of the text's contents in hearing, reading, speaking, and writing. The beginning is best made before the pupil even sees the text. First the teacher explains new expressions in the foreign language and leads the pupils to use them in speech over and over again.[57] Then the students read

---

* In *The Study of Language*, Bloomfield says that "many students of linguistics, including the present writer, have come to believe that the acquisition of a 'reading knowledge' is greatly delayed and that the reader's understanding remains very imperfect unless he has some command of actual speech."[56]

the selection after the teacher and answer questions about the text, first with the book, then without it. At the elementary level, work outside class should be at a minimum, as there is great possibility of error in pronunciation and usage. The safest work is copying the text and sentences from it. Since not much outside work is possible at this stage, eight or nine hours of class work is not too much for the first year or two.[58]

In many instances, however, professors of language continued to teach in the traditional way, and most other linguists of the country remained preoccupied with their theoretical problems in analyzing American Indian languages.[59] Writing in 1945, Bloomfield could still say, "Not one in a hundred of our foreign language teachers has read . . . any respectable book of linguistics."[60] Bloomfield is discussed again in Chapter V in conjunction with the army's World War II Intensive Language Program. Before the war other theories of language teaching emerged, theories that exerted a major influence on actual practice throughout the period and which still play a part in foreign language teaching in the United States.

Until the end of the nineteenth century, the most prevalent system of foreign-language teaching in American universities was the grammar-translation method, based on the principle that understanding a foreign language begins with parallel statements in the native language. Study and memorization of grammar rules was considered the basis for progress in language learning. As each rule was mastered, the students learned vocabulary, lesson by lesson. The vocabulary was then used to translate difficult passages which tested their knowledge of the rules. There was little or no stress on pronunciation or on composition; the chief purpose of this type of language teaching was developing an ability to translate. The main objective remained a knowledge of grammar rules; the application of the rules was often a secondary matter. In criticizing the method, J. C. Catford argues that systems of different languages impose different "grids" on our experience of the world. These grids, distribution of patterns and meanings, are rarely if ever identical. The main fault of the grammar-translation method was that it ignored the different systems among semantically similar structures.[61]

It seemed unimportant that students who devoted years to studying a foreign language were in most cases unable to use it.[62] Little serious effort was made to oppose the traditional method with the application of linguistic studies until the 1920's and the appearance of works tracing the historical doctrines of correctness.[63]

One of the more promising new theories in language teaching was the direct method, which developed first in Europe as a reaction against the grammar-translation method. The new approach emphasized learning by direct contact with the foreign language in meaningful situations. Its central idea was the association of words and sentences with the meaning through demonstrations, dramatizations, pictures, and so forth. More important for its success in the United States than any other individual was François Gouin, a Frenchman who emigrated to America in 1881 and whose book, published in 1880, provided the basis for a great number of government and private manuals and texts on EFL teaching.[64]

According to Gouin, the child's first linguistic exercises are derived at home from the speech of the mother. The material is "prodigiously rich," so rich that when the child crosses the threshold and ventures out, "he is already able to analyze and put into words the great unknown world that lies spread before him."[65] The reason the adult seldom arrives at assimilating other languages is because he seldom thinks of translating these rudimentary series which form what might be called his first words, that is, the first basis of his individuality.

The ear is the most immediate organ of language. "To substitute for it the eye or the hand, as is done in all the schools at the present time, is to commit a capital blunder";[66] the lesson should always be oral before it is visual. A child listens for two years before constructing a phrase and knows the spoken word long before producing it or being able to read it. To learn a language is to "translate into this language not Goethe, not Virgil . . . but the vast book of our individuality." A person must take all of his perceptions one by one and treat them exactly as does the child; "each perception represents not a solitary fact, but a totality, a group of facts more or less extensive."[67] Each chapter of this "individuality" Gouin sees as a "series" of ends, reached by a consecutive number of activities, or means to the ends:

> If I follow the growth of an oak . . . from the time the acorn falls to the ground to the moment when . . . it produces an acorn in its turn, I shall have named all the phenomena of which this tree is the . . . cause. In the history of a single tree I shall have the history of all trees. . . . I shall have nothing more to ask of the dictionary than certain substantives, the names of certain species.[68]

In dealing with the time aspect of tenses, Gouin notes:

> Every time we wish to state, not an abstract idea, but an actual fact which exists in time, we always begin by mentioning or by indicating this time:

Yesterday	Arthur visited a friend.
Last week	Arthur visited a friend.
Last month	Arthur visited a friend.
Last year	Arthur visited a friend.

Compared with *yesterday, today, tomorrow, this morning,* the terms *past, present, future,* are relatively meaningless abstractions that do not help establish understanding.[69]

With the need to present vocabulary in context, the author suggests that words can be taught by drawing. Isolated words are comparable to isolated elements in drawing, for example, a face, or parts of a face. For a word to be rightly used or a figure rightly drawn, both must have a correct relationship to their environment; they must be limited or defined by their environment. Substantives present two diverse characteristics, specific and general. Specific words like *ax* are much more important than general ones like *implement.* It is possible to get along without general terms but not without specific ones, which will have a closely corresponding translation in a foreign language while the general terms like *instrument* or *tool* will seldom find an exact equivalent.

Gouin's pedagogic unit is the theme, a general end accomplished by a series of related acts. Shown here in the accompanying chart is how the author develops one theme, titled "The Maid Chops a Log of Wood." Remember, he demonstrates the theme as clearly as possible without recourse to the printed word.

On reaching the final answer, "the end is attained. The exercise is finished—the theme is complete."[71] Following the main development of the theme there are also items for substitution:

THE MAID CHOPS A LOG OF WOOD

To chop a log of wood, we require a hatchet. Therefore,
first of all—she goes to seek
the hatchet.

Then what does she do?	*She takes a log of wood.*
Then what does she do?	*She goes up to the chopping block.*
Then what does she do?	*She kneels down near the block.*
Then what does she do?	*She places the wood on the block.*
Then what does she do?	*She raises the hatchet.*
What follows?	*The hatchet cleaves the air.*
Then what happens?	*The hatchet strikes the wood.*
Then what happens?	*The blade buries itself in the wood.*
And then?	*The blade cleaves the wood.*
And then?	*The two pieces fall to the ground.*
And then?	*The maid picks up the pieces.*
And then?	*She chops them again and again to the desired size.*
And then?	*She stands up again.*
And then?	*She carries the hatchet back to its place.*[70]

---

1. maid (housewife, cook, servant, domestic, girl, woman, person, she)
2. chopping block (block, log, billet, article, thing, it, object)
3. place (right place, proper place, spot, corner, post, position,
location)
4. blade (edge, cutting edge, sharp edge, keen edge, iron, steel,
metal, it)

5. hatchet (ax, wood ax, chopper, chopping knife, cleaver, cutter, bill, instrument, tool)

Lexical analysis of the lesson shows that the main body presents sixteen different verbs, twelve nouns, three adjectives, five prepositions, six pronouns, a total of forty-two separate words. The forty additional words in the appendix give a sum total of eighty-two words.

A problem that continues to plague EFL programs is the number of hours and general amount of time needed for a complete language course. Whether or not we agree with it, Gouin's projection offers a specific answer to the problem. A total course will contain about fifty to sixty chapters, each with a general series consisting of fifty to eighty separate themes or exercises. There are about twenty-five sentences in a theme. On the average, five themes are taught an hour. Figuring eighty themes per chapter and fifty chapters, we reach a figure of eight hundred hours. Gouin adds another hundred hours for unforeseen possibilities, which brings the course to a grand total of nine hundred.[72] Gouin leaves unanswered the question of apportioning this figure among weeks and years. Perhaps nine hundred hours seems high, but the figure does fall within the range found in the army Intensive Language Program of World War II (see Chapter V) as well as in many EFL programs today.

Gouin developed the theme approach from analysis of his own efforts to learn a foreign language. Although techniques have been considerably refined, his basic philosophy still has much to recommend it:

1. The ear, not the eye, is the instrument for learning to speak a foreign language.

2. An understanding of isolated words, even all those in the dictionary, does not ensure the understanding of, even less an ability to use, spoken words.

3. To ensure such ability, a larger unit than the word is necessary.

4. The meaning of an expression must be made clear by associating the sentence with the idea represented.

5. An understanding of oral symbols is the basis for reading and writing and must precede them.

Gouin's work was developed and widely disseminated by Henry H. Goldberger, who lectured in methods of EFL teaching at Teachers College, Columbia, in the 1920's. Through Goldberger, the Gouin method became the most popular approach to EFL teaching in the early part of the century.

According to Goldberger, grave mistakes have been made in the past in the choice of lesson material. Too much emphasis has been placed on literary features of the English language and too little on the practical English that pupils need for their home, working, or community life. As a corrective, Goldberger suggests subject matter from the students' everyday experiences. Each lesson is organized around a central theme. In the early lessons this central idea or theme should be developed in not over fifteen sentences, which follow one another according to a logical sequence of time, with provision for natural resting places, for example, fifteen sentences in groups of five each. No more than ten sentences in a theme can be memorized to advantage.

In preparing a theme, the teacher selects an ultimate purpose or action, such as "To Visit the Doctor" or "Going to Work," then constructs a series of sentences, each describing a certain act leading up to the accomplishment of the final activity. For teaching the theme, the teacher uses the oral approach and conveys meaning by dramatizations (action, gesture, the play of features), objects, and pictures. Goldberger suggests the following:

1. Question the pupils, requiring answers that use words taught in the sentences of the various themes.

2. Let the pupils question each other about the lessons.

3. Give commands orally or on the blackboard and have students execute them, then tell what they did.

4. Dramatize universal activities and have the students tell what you did.

5. Design sound drills that are centered around the words appearing in the themes.[73]

The first steps are especially valuable with beginners, when the teacher and pupils cannot understand each other. However, shortly after the pupils can speak a little English, there is less need for objectifying experience.

Goldberger suggests there should be little time spent on rules and grammatical definitions, with most of the class devoted to drilling the structures in exercises such as pattern practice. In the sentence "I wrote him yesterday," students substitute other pronouns for *I*, other time expressions for *yesterday*. Teaching procedure should place the main emphasis on oral instruction and practice of speaking rather than relying on the printed page.[74]

Goldberger distinguishes two kinds of writing: as a means —formal exercises in copying, dictation, filling in blanks, and paraphrasing, which are necessary for drill—and composition—writing for the purpose of communicating thoughts to others. He observes that the great mass of immigrants have far less need for writing in English than do native Americans.[75] For foreign students studying at institutions of higher learning, the need to develop writing skills would be essential. Spelling would have value only in relation to writing. As for pronunciation, Goldberger found that immigrants tended to regard it as an embellishment rather than a necessity. He feels that even though a certain amount of pronunciation work is necessary—at least work in minimal pairs for distinguishing meaning—the great amount of time necessary for adult pronunciation is better spent elsewhere.[76]

Table A
Typical Time Distribution

Subject	Time
Reading	40 minutes
Copying	15 minutes
Dictation	20 minutes
Spelling	10 minutes
Civics (reading)	20 minutes
Conversation	15 minutes
Phonics	10 minutes

From a study of sample time programs of public English courses for immigrants, Goldberger found that in beginning classes more time was given to reading and writing than to oral work. A typical distribution in a school where English is taught two hours a night, three nights a week, is shown in Table A. In contrast, the time division of a lesson suggested by Goldberger is shown in Table B.

Not all linguists showed complete acceptance of the direct method. Henry Sweet (1845–1912), the great English phonetician and language scholar, points out several limitations. The direct method presupposes the same process in first- and second-language learning. In learning the native language, we begin young and devote all our time to it. The mind is blank and free from all linguistic or associative inter-

Table B. Goldberger Suggested Time Division

Subject	Period		
	2–hour	1½–hour	1–hour
Conversation	20 minutes	15 minutes	10 minutes
Theme	35	30	20
Word Drill	10	5	5*
Sentence Drill	10	5	5
Writing	30	25	20
Incidental Reading	10	5	5*
Physical Training†	5	5	5

* On alternate lessons.
† To relax in class and also teach parts of the body and directions.

ference. New words and ideas are learned simultaneously. However, the learning process is very slow. For the more mature student learning a second language, the power of imitation has decreased, especially in pronunciation. But the mind is formed, capable of generalization and abstraction, with infinitely greater knowledge of things and ideas. Increasing maturity brings greater powers of concentration and methodological perseverance. Except for first-language interference, these more than compensate for the disadvantages. Thus, the natural or direct method puts the adult in the position of an infant, without allowing him to use his own special abilities.[78]

Actually, Sweet's approach resembles the direct method by insisting on spoken forms and use of the foreign language in class. It differs sharply in emphasizing pronunciation and phonetics as the main focus. Under the direct method, Sweet objected, words and concepts dealt almost entirely with the concrete and objective world, while excluding most abstract and subjective elements of the language. Moreover, it had strong grammatical limitations, practicing only principal sentences in the present tense and only first- or third-person verbs.[79]

In contrast, Sweet offers certain principles for language analysis and language teaching. Certain of these principles have gained an important place in applied linguistics, while others have been superseded. Sweet makes five general observations:

1. From the practical and scientific point of view, the sentence, not the word, is the unit of language.

2. The sentence is to the text as the word is to the sentence: both are relations of context. Sentences and words may have ambiguous grammatical form and meaning when detached from their larger units.

3. Therefore, language should be studied through connected texts, accompanied by grammatical analysis.

4. Since grammatical rules must be illustrated and justified by separate sentences, one should choose sentences that are contextual, that is, meaningful within themselves.

5. The psychological foundation of language learning is the law of association. The process of language learning is that of forming these associations.[80]

In addition, he suggests several stages in language learning:

1. *Mechanical*—a thorough mastery of pronunciation, which presupposes a general knowledge of phonetics. Phonetic exercises should include some of the most necessary and frequent elements of grammar and vocabulary plus a few indispensable idioms. When some progress has been made in the first stage, a few short texts for reading should be introduced, still without any grammatical analysis.

2. *Grammatical stage*—presupposes a complete mastery of pronunciation and control over a certain amount of grammatical and lexical material. Texts are chosen to embody grammatical categories of an *increasing order of difficulty.* Vocabulary is expanded but is still completely subordinate to grammar.

3. *Idiomatic and lexical stage*—items are learned chiefly through reading texts. Words and phrases necessary for the most basic and necessary ideas are introduced. Total command at this stage should be about 3,000 words.

4. *Literary*—actual reading of unmodified literature, going from simple prose gradually to higher prose and poetry. With relatively unphonetic scripts such as French and English, the learner first begins to acquire nomic, or graphic, spelling at this stage. With languages that are written more phonetically, nomic spelling can be started earlier.

Sweet returns constantly to the spoken language, urging that foreigners be taught the reduced forms, such as *can't,* since they will encounter them more frequently.[81] His *Primer of Spoken English* attempts to provide "a faithful picture—a phonetic photograph—of educated spoken English as distinguished from vulgar and provincial English on the one hand and literary English on the other."[82] Passing briefly over points adequately treated in conventional grammars, the author gives "greater prominence to such totally new subjects as gradation, sentence-stress,"[83] emphasizing the phonetic aspects of morphology and syntax. For example, discussing noun plural forms, he lists /-s, -z, -iz/, plus such forms as <oxen>, <children>, <sheep>, <feet>.

Certain of Sweet's observations relate to newer theories.

Note the following and its implications for transformational and tagmemic analysis:

> Syntactic rules are . . . more perfect than those which deal only with forms of words. Many syntactic rules hardly admit of exceptions; when there are exceptions, they are the result of crossing by other syntactic rules, or . . . the exception is one for which a clear reason can be given.[84]

All rules covering a large category indicate how far it is possible to carry the analogy of a particular form. When dealing with greater complexity and irregularity, one can design elaborate rules with many exceptions or present only the rules that are most efficient. "A great part of all languages consists of a limited number of natural sentences, only some of which admit being formed a priori and freely modified by the substitution of other words."[85]

Sweet distinguishes between lexical and grammatical words. For example, in *the disobedience of man, man* and *disobedience* are lexical, while *of* belongs to grammar, performing the same function as *-s* genitive. Grammar deals with material subject to general laws. Other phenomena belong to the dictionary. However, criteria for determining lexical and grammatical categories differ between languages. In classical Arabic, for example, the formation of roots is included in the grammar.[86]

Henry Sweet influenced most late-nineteenth-century writers on language teaching. The International Phonetic Alphabet was based on his "Broad Romic."[87] In fact, all of his work added significantly to the scientific study of language.

Another influential linguistic scholar of the period was Otto Jespersen (1860–1943), whose book, *How to Teach a*

Foreign Language, is cited in many language-teaching texts of the times. Reading it further reveals some of the origins of modern practice. Convinced of the need for a contextual approach to language learning, Jespersen states:

> One cannot say anything sensible with mere lists of words, indeed not even disconnected sentences ought to be used. . . . For there is generally just as little connection between them as there would be in a newspaper if the same line were read all the way across from column to column.[88]

However, he sees no danger in using really self-interpreting sentences, such as "There are twelve months in a year." Like Gouin, he finds a relationship between drawing and vocabulary and suggests that the teacher put the names of several different items on the blackboard, have the students draw them in detail, then explain their drawings to the class.[89]

Jespersen regards grammatical propositions as abstractions which are often difficult even for the experts and therefore far beyond the grasp of the pupils. "One cannot really begin to learn the grammar of a language until one knows the language itself."[90] By drilling a pattern in isolation, the student learns to produce it mechanically but is unable to use it in different situations. As a corrective, Jespersen recommends pattern practice. Conjugating a verb alone in all its forms is sheer drudgery, but the exercise becomes more interesting and more beneficial when a whole sentence is used, for example, in the sentence "I gave Bill a dollar," substituting words for *a dollar*, *I*, and *gave*. Jespersen, however, retains several old-fashioned pedagogical approaches, such as picking out certain grammatical items in a reading passage and commenting on them.

Nevertheless, much of his work represents the best in nine-teenth-century language teaching.

Following is a sequence for designing and presenting vocab-ulary and structure items:

1. Construct a short passage containing the lexical and grammatical items you want to teach.

2. When asking questions about it, deviate as little as pos-sible from the words of the text.

3. The first few times the exercise is used, the teacher should direct the same questions to several students.

4. Ask as many questions as possible.

5. As time goes by, the teacher may depart from the text by asking students about their own affairs outside of class, still using the specific lexicon and structures as a peg.

6. Have the students ask each other the same kind of ques-tions.[91]

With one exception, this method represents some of the most advanced approaches used today. The difference is that in modern practice the whole passage is presented orally, one sentence at a time, so that there is only an oral-aural stimulus. This procedure will be examined more fully in the section on current methods in Chapter VI.

Jespersen notes that sooner or later pupils should write origi-nal compositions in the foreign language, but finds one danger in this. By using a slender supply of fairly vague ex-pressions, students often conceal their difficulties. The solu-tion, according to Jespersen, is in having the teacher assign topics at a low level of abstraction, for example, events that he has discussed in class or a renarration of an episode in a novel or in history. In this way, it is easy to recognize the student's structural problems.

There are several ways of presenting foreign-language material, with concomitant advantages and disadvantages:

1. *Everything is presented orally.* With no recourse to the printed word, the student avoids the confusion of written symbols. This method resembles the child's learning process and is desirable only when there is one or very few pupils, when students are still quite young, and when there is ample time. Its chief disadvantage is the great amount of time required. For this reason, purely oral work in schools is possible only as a short preliminary course before passing over to some form of writing.

2. *Orthography alone.* The difference between orthography and pronunciation is usually great. The endless need for corrections created by such an approach is extremely discouraging, especially to beginning students.

3. *Orthography and phonetic transcription.* Pupils are taught traditional spelling from the start but at the same time are given phonetic transcription, either in a glossary or in the entire passage. The problem with this approach is that less intelligent pupils confuse the two systems and as a result learn neither orthography nor pronunciation very well.

4. *Phonetic transcription alone.* Nothing else is used for some time. The pupils become quite familiar with the sound system and structural features of the language. Texts are thus easier to learn than if orthography had to be mastered at the same time. Connected texts are particularly helpful for explicating combined (sandhi) forms. The length of time for a purely phonetic approach depends on age, maturity, and the

number of hours available for the course. In a two-year class meeting two hours a week, Jespersen spends the entire first year using the all-phonetic approach. He recommends continuing with phonetic transcription as long as possible.[92]

One of the leading EFL specialists in the first half of the twentieth century was Harold Palmer,[93] who developed the principles of Sweet and Jespersen into a formal detailed program.[94] Working in the Department of Phonetics in the University of London, 1914–21, he evolved his oral method of teaching languages, with an emphasis on phonetic training for language teachers. Throughout his work are some extremely perceptive observations on language structure, plus a variety of oral drills that are the precursors of pattern practice.

According to Palmer, the oral method involves "learning to speak a foreign language without reading, without writing, without theory, and without translation, by dint of listening to the teacher speaking and responding to what he says."[95] While the oral method does not represent the entire language course, "it is the most powerful help towards our assimilating the material of both the spoken and written languages."[96] "The results obtained by oral and conversational work are almost invariably superior, never inferior, to those attained by the more traditional methods of book-work and pen-work."[97] As an illustration, Palmer cites a group of Belgian refugee children returning from England after World War I, "in possession of an English speech hardly to be distinguished from the speech of English children of their own age." Most of the exceptions, those who did not learn, were among older children who had developed their intelligence and were forced to use it as a means of language learning. They were given considerable visual material and were taught to analyze, to translate. This approach affected their work adversely; it "interfered with the process by which nature causes us to assimilate and to remember."[98]

According to Palmer, the best method for language learning is one that makes no demands on the student's capacities for reasoning, analysis, or theorizing. Instead of selecting and adapting previously acquired habits connected with the first language, the student must form new habits. The conscious use of one's intellectual powers Palmer refers to as the studial capacity. "Whenever we are distinctly conscious of the words and constructions we are using . . . whenever we come to understand a sentence by analyzing it, or to utter a sentence by piecing it together as we go on, we are working by the process of studial order."[99] Studial items include such things as conversions (affirmative, negative, or question) and all methods that involve the eye. Though Palmer favors the direct method as a means of establishing unconscious oral habits, he feels that the studial capacity is essential for certain reasons. When the written language is highly unphonetic, as English is, there are virtually two separate languages. As a result, it is necessary, at a given time, to employ devices such as dictation, reading aloud, and spelling.

At the elementary level, the teacher must retrain the student in how to learn. He must instill habits of correct observation, of listening, of using his capacities for unconscious assimilation, and of forming direct associations. The student must learn to break the "isolating" habits of learning individual words instead of groups of words. Palmer goes on to enumerate several specific principles of language study:

1. *Initial preparation.* The teacher must awaken the non-studial capacities of the student, who should not be allowed to focus on structures but must keep his attention on the subject matter.

2. *Habit-forming and habit-adapting.* Parrot-like repetition of the same sentence, over and over, can be dulling. However, repetition, "in the sense ascribed to it by psychologists, simply means having many separate occasions to hear, to see, to utter, or to write a given word or sentence. The object of most language teaching exercises, drills, and devices invented or developed in recent years is precisely to ensure proper repetition in attractive and interesting ways."[100] There are several methods of developing these unconscious habit-forming powers:[101]

   a. *Ear-training exercises.* The student learns to perceive correctly what he hears.

   b. *Articulation exercises.* The vocal organs are taught to make the right sort of muscular effort.

   c. *Exercises in mimicry.* The student learns to imitate or reproduce words or a string of words uttered by the teacher.

   d. *Exercises in immediate comprehension.* The student comes to grasp the general sense of what he hears, without mental translation or analysis.

3. *Gradation.* In this context the word signifies a way of organizing material so that the student passes from the known to the unknown in easy stages. This can be done in several ways.

   a. *Ears before eyes.* All new material is first introduced in its oral form.

   b. *Reception before production.* The student should have

ample opportunity of hearing the sound, word, or word group before being called on to produce it.

c. *Oral repetition before reading.*

d. *Chorus work before individual work.* Choral repetition gives the student greater confidence and also a certain mastery of material.

e. *Drill work before free work.*

4. *Proportion.* There must be proper attention to different skills (understanding, speaking, reading, writing) as well as to various branches of study (phonetics, orthography, morphology, syntax, semantics). Each of the four skills requires special methods of teaching. Mastering one skill does not automatically mean the student has mastered another.

5. *Concreteness.* Structure and meaning should proceed from the concrete to the abstract. Concreteness is the chief determining factor in the choice of early vocabulary; the most demonstrable words and compounds should be taught first.

Several valuable concepts appear in Palmer's studies, for example, his distinction between memorized and constructed matter. "Each unit has either been memorized by the user integrally as it stands or else is composed by the user from smaller and previously memorized units."[102] Memorized matter includes everything learned as a unit, whether syllables, words, word groups, sentences, or whole passages. "Most things we utter or write come into the category of constructed matter,"[103] that is, combinations of already learned units, which join together to form sentences. The author does not work out the applications of his concept, but they can be seen in the later development of tagmemics and the use of structural slots, which are discussed in Chapter VI.

Palmer also contrasts receptive and productive work. In elementary classes, the teacher should make a distinction, spending considerably more time on receptive work, since it is hard for the elementary student to focus on both. Either the student concentrates on what he hears and cannot prepare a response, or he thinks only of the answer and cannot hear correctly. "The consciousness of being expected to produce, at all costs, some sort of answer, is responsible for many linguistic failures."[104] By concentrating solely on listening, the beginner can hear and observe correctly. Some kind of response is desirable as a check on the student's concentration, for example, having him answer or mark a printed question sheet. Such exercises are especially suitable for the language laboratory. Unlimited size is also an advantage of a class designed only for receptive work, while Palmer suggests a maximum of twelve for classes with question and answer work and a maximum of four for conversation classes. The army Specialized Training Program, discussed in Chapter V, had large classes for grammatical explanations in the native language, English, and small ones for drilling in the target languages.

In his *Grammar of Spoken English*, Palmer states that the function of a grammar book is to "furnish the student with a selection of those categories which will enable him to perform the greatest number of substitutions."[105] Intended primarily for adult foreign students and teachers of spoken English, the book contains the kind of English used by the average educated speaker. "In pronunciation, in the choice of words and expressions, and in grammatical usage, it [the text] represents . . . the type of dialect . . . of the majority of those with whom he [the author] has generally come into contact."[106]

In addition to words with lexical meaning, there are those

that only express relationships between different parts of the sentence; they have syntactic or grammatical functions. The author uses the term *alogism* to designate such syntactic and morphological devices as word order, inflection, intonation, and affixes. In other words, an alogism represents the lexical function of certain syntactic relationships, for example, the substitution of *fruit tree* for *tree which bears fruit,* with primary stress on *fruit.* Similarly, English uses the terms *coffee cup, letter box,* and *post office,* for the French *tasse à café, boîte aux lettres,* and *bureau de poste.* The French *boîte à allumete* is equivalent to the English *match box,* the relational idea expressed in French by *à,* in English by word order and also by stress.[107] In another example, English *he will come* is expressed in French by *il viendra,* the English structure word *will* expressed by the French inflection of *venir.*

Ideally, lexical words would be treated in dictionaries, structure words and their alogistic equivalents in grammar books. Practically, this is neither feasible nor desirable, since it is often difficult to distinguish between them and they often shift categories. The concept of the word presents problems when moving from one language to another. Why, for example, should the French *quioque* be one word while *bien que* is two? In order to avoid confusion, Palmer urges replacing *word* with the terms *monolog, polylog,* and *miolog,* which he defines as follows:

1. *Monolog.* Words considered as conventional orthographical units by virtue of being written in one piece.

2. *Polylog.* Two or more monologs semantically equivalent to a monolog, for example, *in case, of course, in spite of, on Sunday, during winter, hardly ever, leave off, for a long time.*

3. *Miolog.* Units such as affixes and the more concrete inflections such as *-ly, -ment, -ed, -graph, poly-, con-, ortho-, re-,* and *-'s.*[108]

⚜ IV ⚜

The Growth of English as a Foreign Language, 1880-1940

THE DEVELOPMENT of EFL courses in the United States was a response to the needs of many groups of people who required knowledge of a new language to cope successfully with the demands of their environment: immigrants, refugees, and students, all traveling thousands of miles to fulfill different dreams. The group immediately responsible for the origin of courses in English as a foreign language was composed of immigrants, over thirty million entering the New World between 1815 and 1914.[1]

In 1860, out of a total foreign-born population of 4.1 million, the majority were concentrated in New York, Pennsylvania, Ohio, Illinois, Wisconsin, and Massachusetts. Foreign-born made up almost half the populations of New York, Chicago, Cincinnati, Milwaukee, Detroit, and San Francisco. In 1910, 23 per cent of the urban United States population was foreign-born.

From the beginning of the colonial period, English had been the first language of a great number of immigrants, and later arrivals thus accepted the responsibility of learning it. Nevertheless, before 1865, especially in farming areas and small settlements, native languages prevailed. The man of the house acquired a few English phrases, but not the wife, isolated on her farm. Moreover, the free school, ill equipped, ill staffed, and lacking materials for language teaching, usually proved inadequate to the immigrants' needs. In fact, many groups developed their own schools, often organized by the church. But increasing contact with English-speaking Americans placed a greater burden on the immigrant's language. English experienced a further wave of prestige, partly because of the presence of one million English immigrants who, with their greater initial resources and a knowledge of the language, usually reached higher levels in community affairs.

Other factors as well exerted their influence. In 1860 the United States was not a nation but a congeries of small ethnic regions. The Civil War changed this situation. For one thing, it improved the immigrant's economic position enormously. The Panic of 1857 had ruined the grain market, and stocks had been piling high in farm buildings. With the sudden great wartime demand, prices shot up. "The poor immigrant of 1857 became the rich farmer of 1865."[2] Even more important, 500,000 foreign-born volunteers fought in the Civil War. For four years mothers and fathers found themselves a part of the struggle, which created in them new attitudes toward the society their sons were fighting to preserve.

Foreigners reached America in three great movements. The first, five million strong, between 1815 and 1860, came predominantly from England, Germany, Scandinavia, Switzerland, and Holland. Between 1860 and 1890, another ten million arrived, chiefly from the same areas. But the fifteen million who landed between 1890 and 1914 were "strangers," mostly from Austria-Hungary, Russia, Greece, Rumania, and

Turkey. Largely uneducated and illiterate, these new Americans provided the greatest challenge to the melting pot. As their presence loomed larger and larger in the population, government, industry, and the immigrants themselves began to recognize that they had much to learn of the new way of life and that the most direct way to learn it was through a knowledge of English.

The majority of foreigners unable to speak English were found in the northeastern states, more than two-thirds in New York, Pennsylvania, Illinois, Massachusetts, Ohio, New Jersey, Texas, Wisconsin, and Michigan. All of these states except Texas were north of the Ohio River and east of the Mississippi. Seventeen per cent of the immigrants arriving in 1893, besides being unable to speak English, were illiterate in any language. The figure rose to 30 per cent in 1915, with the post–World War I figure dropping to 5 per cent as a result of the literacy test.

For a long time, many groups, including labor and patriotic societies, worked to limit immigration, especially of people from southern and east-central Europe. In 1917, on the eve of the war, the restrictionists were able to force an immigration law through Congress over President Wilson's veto. Among other things, the law provided for the exclusion of adult aliens unable to read a short passage in English or some other language, except for illiterate members of a family or persons fleeing religious persecutions. In 1924 the Johnson-Reed Act, based on national origins, further reduced the admission of people from southern and eastern Europe.

By 1900 the need for "Americanizing" these immigrants with their alien traditions and poor education began to loom larger. Public and private agencies arose, designed to help the immigrant adapt to American life. Among the most important aspects of Americanization was the teaching of English as a foreign language.

Gradually, especially in large cities, public institutions introduced courses for educating the immigrant. Among private organizations most concerned with the problem were the Immigrants Protective League in Chicago, the Young Men's Christian Association (YMCA), and the North American Civic League for Immigrants. Founded in the spring of 1918, the Civic League was devoted to protecting new immigrants and to promoting means for their assimilation, including learning the English language. To this end it worked with public authorities to establish and develop classes in EFL. Another group, the YMCA, conducted as many as three thousand different EFL classes in 1917. During the war, it received a government commission to conduct classes for non-English-speaking draftees. The period 1910–20 also saw the increase of public-corporate activity in teaching EFL, in which the public agency shared the burden of education with the corporation.

After 1915 the problem of Americanization and EFL teaching received increasing attention from school administrators, as it came to be recognized that a distinct pedagogy and methodology were needed. More and more methods courses began to appear in college offerings.* Although teaching methods varied, the trend was toward the Gouin approach.

It is difficult to generalize about the problems and programs

---

* For the years 1915–16, several cities reported special training courses for teachers of EFL, notably Albany, Buffalo, Rochester, and St. Louis. Teachers College, Columbia University, offered summer courses in EFL methods and was probably the pioneer in the field.

of individual states. Furthermore, such an analysis is somewhat wide of the mark in this study of language teaching. Those who would pursue the topic are referred to Appendix 1, which discusses developments in various states, and to Appendix 2, which provides an analysis of the most popular EFL texts used during the period.

The tradition of foreign students studying in American colleges is older than commonly believed. Francisco de Miranda came from Venezuela to study at Yale in 1784, and Yung Wing was the first Chinese to graduate from an American university, also Yale, in 1854.[3] In parts of South America, notably Colombia, the student movement to Europe and the United States dated especially from the Colombian Revolution of 1903. Peace brought with it foreign capital, mostly British, and English began to replace French in the language curriculum. The teaching of English was "directly responsible for the sending of many Colombians to the United States."[4] Still, before World War I, the number of foreign students remained relatively low. In 1911 there were 3,645, and in 1913, 4,222 in 275 United States colleges and universities.[5] There were several reasons for the relatively small number of foreign students before World War I. Geographical distance was one, and another was the advanced position of European universities and the shortage of graduate schools in the United States as centers of productive scholarship and research. At this time, moreover, the United States government followed a rather strong isolationist policy, reflected partly in the lack of interest shown by American institutions in foreign students. Very little was done in the way of scholarships or provisions for orientation. "At a time when many countries were signing voluminous cultural agreements providing for the exchange of students, the government of the United States avoided even this area of 'entangling alliances,' leaving by default to private agencies the task of furthering the cause of cultural exchange."[6] But private institutions did become interested. By 1925 more than 115 private organizations had been established in the United States concerned in some way with the exchange of students and teachers. One of these was the Institute of International Education, begun in 1919 to further the concept of international understanding by many means, including selection and orientation of foreign students.

After World War I, many of the older countries, "dissatisfied with their own traditions of education and looking toward increasing opportunities in education, and the more backward countries, looking for new foundations for modern systems of education, began to turn their attention to American education."[7] By 1921 there were 6,488 foreign students in American colleges, with the figure rising to 10,033 by 1929. The majority of these students came from non-English-speaking countries, and many needed work in English before undertaking a regular course of study. Gradually the problem came to be recognized at the university level. In 1923 a questionnaire was sent to four hundred colleges by the Commission on the Survey of Foreign Students in the United States. Returns from 110 college administrators revealed only two institutions without "provisions for special classes."[8] Harvard offered English classes for foreign students beginning in 1927;[9] George Washington University and Cornell offered classes starting in 1931.

But the program that showed the fullest development in this early period was one at Columbia University, its first course appearing in 1911. By 1920 the offering had grown to six ungraded one-year courses. The year 1925 saw the addition of an intermediate course, and by 1935 the curriculum had expanded to include three separate levels. In addition, from 1923 to 1938 the International Institute of Teachers College, Columbia, experimented with special courses and programs for foreign students. Besides classes in EFL, Teachers College developed courses in American civilization, which provided an orientation to American values and institutions as well as further practice in English.

During this period, however, most college offerings in EFL were limited to occasional courses that never really evolved into integrated programs. The first such program did not appear until 1940, with the emergence of the English Language Institute of the University of Michigan.

Diverse political and economic forces influenced the amount and direction of EFL teaching in the period 1880–1940. For example, the campaign to Americanize the immigrant did not really begin until 1915, when public offices started formulating programs. Before this time, neither the Bureau of Naturalization nor the Bureau of Education had paid much attention to the problem. Before World War I, the nationalistic element in American education was low. The war created a strong awareness of the need for such an element. "No nation," urges Frank Thompson,[10] "can be secure in peace or competent in war without guarantees as to the loyalty and unity of its citizens, and these matters cannot be taken for granted, as we have taken them in the past.... America, with its diversified population, will surely be alert to the need of nationalization through the schools, as perhaps the strongest lesson which the war has taught us."[11]

During the war, immigration was virtually halted.[12] In

1920 it began to flow again, but the Immigration Law of 1929 attempted to choke it off. However, before the law had time to alter the pattern of immigration, the depression reduced the influx to a mere trickle. Throughout the depression decade, most quotas remained unfilled. Fewer than 350,000 Europeans entered the United States between 1931 and 1940, and with a certain number leaving each year, the net gain was negligible. Under public pressure, President Hoover ordered a stronger enforcement of the Immigration Law toward the end of his term in office, prohibiting people likely to become a public charge. This policy, continued by Franklin D. Roosevelt until 1937, assured the exclusion of all but the most prosperous Europeans.

Starting in 1933, a considerable number of refugees began to arrive from Nazi Germany, particularly after 1938, following Hitler's union with Austria and the increasing anti-Semitic campaigns. However, depression legislation greatly restricted this number, and many were unable to escape. After 1940 the German quota was unblocked.

The composition of these refugees differed strongly from that of earlier movements. For one thing, the newer arrivals were largely, though not completely, Jewish, mostly middle-class, urban, white-collar, professional, and business people, who found the language barrier a greater obstacle to employment than did farmers and laborers. Public and private agencies aided the recent arrivals in pursuing their education by referring them to English classes offered by boards of education and various colleges and universities.[13] In a survey of refugees, language was regarded as the most important problem with 42.8 per cent of the men and 49.3 per cent of the women.[14] Among the main problems in learning English

79

were listed colloquialisms and slang. One refugee said his greatest problem was learning the "slanguage" in addition to the language. Others stressed difficulties in such areas as pronunciation. "The aspirations of the refugees themselves drove them to strive for language facility . . . they have not been content with a superficial knowledge of the English language, but have been anxious to master it and use it like educated native Americans."[15] The accompanying chart shows the conclusions of a survey by the Committee for Study of Recent Immigration from Europe, covering 1933–44, comparing refugee immigrants with earlier arrivals.[16]

There had never been a quota on immigrants from the Western Hemisphere. After 1924 they formed a much larger proportion than before. Mexican immigration, greatly reduced during the depression, began to burgeon during the war. By 1945 there were 2.5 million Mexicans in the United States. Originally concentrated in the Southwest as migrant workers, they fanned out with the mechanization of agriculture, eventually settling in such places as Chicago, Toledo, and Detroit. Like the Mexicans, the Puerto Ricans have had free entry into the United States since 1900, when Puerto Rico became an unincorporated territory. The numbers of Puerto Rican immigrants were quite small until 1920 and the end of mass immigration from Europe. With increasing population pressure, the island was soon unable to support itself, and Puerto Ricans began to move north. The depression halted the flow. In 1940 there were only 70,000 on the mainland. But the war and postwar prosperity brought increasing numbers. By 1957 there were 550,000 in New York and 175,000 in Chicago, Philadelphia, and a number of smaller industrial centers in the Northeast.

REFUGEE IMMIGRANTS

Recent Arrivals

1. Came primarily to escape persecution.
2. Few planned to return to their homeland.
3. Mainly middle and upper class.
4. Mainly business, professional, and white-collar movement; an unusually large number of intellectuals.
5. The majority were educated above elementary school.
6. Chiefly from cities, especially large cities.
7. Cosmopolitan outlook; widely traveled; familiar with languages other than their own.
8. Occasionally came with means.
9. Sought the more desirable types of jobs.
10. Learned English rapidly; dissatisfied with a superficial knowledge of it.

Early Arrivals

1. Came primarily for economic reasons.
2. Many intended to return.
3. Mainly lower and middle class.
4. Mostly peasants, laborers, and artisans; few intellectuals.
5. Most had elementary school background or less; few college or professional school graduates.
6. Chiefly from rural areas and small towns.
7. Seldom traveled beyond their region or country; unfamiliar with other languages.
8. Seldom came with means.
9. Accepted less desirable types of jobs.
10. Acquired English slowly; did not seek to master it.

After the war, the increase of foreign students from non-English-speaking countries carried the problems of EFL teaching to the college level. This problem will be studied in the next chapter. However, the need remained in other areas. As we have seen, the expanding postwar economy attracted people, especially from high-quota countries such as England and Germany. In 1946 the "War Brides and Fiancées" Act allowed 150,000 wives and fiancées and 25,000 children in during the five years after the war. A 1947 amendment to the original law permitted the entry of 5,000 Chinese. Although opposition to admitting European refugees was very strong, especially among congressmen from the South and the Middle West, they still trickled in. Most displaced persons were from low-quota countries, and only 41,000 entered between 1946 and 1948. The Displaced Persons Act of 1948, amended in 1950, provided for the admission of 400,000 refugees in the next four-year period, 1948–52.[17] In spite of the westward movement of people fleeing Communist countries, the majority of refugees were settled by 1952. However, overpopulation plus continuing political persecution kept up the pressure, and Congress passed the Refugee Relief Act in 1953, authorizing the admission of 214,000 persons during the next forty-one-month period.

V

Modern Foreign-Language Programs in the Early 1940's

EFL TEACHING up to World War II developed sporadically and reflected little of the linguistic theory that had begun to emerge between 1925 and 1940. All this changed radically as a result of the war and America's growth as a world power offering an advanced new technology that attracted students from throughout the world. Probably the greatest influence in bringing linguistic theory to bear on the problems of language teaching was the giant operation carried out by the armed forces, the attempt to equip a rather insular people with an understanding of foreign cultures and languages. Other programs, such as the work of the English Language Institute in the University of Michigan and of Wilson's Teacher's College were instrumental in the development of EFL teaching.

The intensive foreign language programs of the army and navy were based in part on certain theories and practices existing before the war. Actually, the army informant technique of having small drill sessions was taken over and further developed from the discoveries of Franz Boas, who, along with scholars like Sapir and Bloomfield, formed the Linguistic Society of America in 1923. In the late 1930's they began to

apply their findings to the problem of language instruction*
and introduced certain basic innovations:

1. Students should spend most of the time imitating a native
speaker in small sessions.
2. There should be fifteen to twenty contact hours a week
instead of three or four.
3. The study of grammar per se has a subordinate place.
4. Reading and writing should not interfere with learning
the spoken language. They should be used when the language
is written phonetically. When it is not, a simplified form of
spelling should be employed.

The war brought a sudden demand for instruction in languages seldom taught previously. The linguists, who were
consulted on methods of teaching, applied the same descriptive techniques in preparing materials as they had used in
their earlier study of languages. These included a native informant, phonemic transcription, and the emphasis of speech
over writing. The Army Specialized Training Program
(ASTP) grew out of materials prepared by the Intensive Language Program of the American Council of Learned Societies.
For several years the council had been carrying on special programs and experiments in language teaching, using intensive
methods and focusing on oral skills. The suggested minimum
time for the ACLS course was ten hours a week, with twenty-
five hours of classwork and supervised study as optimum for
a course of three or more months.[2] In practice, the ACLS
usually ran two or three six-week sessions with short intervals.

---

* "Bloomfield," says Paul F. Angiolillo, "more than any other individual,
had a profound and direct influence on the principles and methods of teaching under the Intensive Language Program."[1]

Conceived as an activity occupying the student full time, courses often worked out to fifteen hours of classroom instruction, fifteen hours of drill with a native speaker, and twenty to thirty hours of individual preparation per week.[3]

From this emerged the ASTP, developed by a group of linguists under Henry Lee Smith, who produced a series of teaching materials, including manuals, dictionaries, and records. The objective of such a program was to train, in several months, men who could act as interpreters and perform other wartime tasks in which a knowledge of the foreign language would be extremely important. The first ASTP courses began in April, 1943. By the end of the year, fifteen thousand trainees were studying languages in fifty-five colleges and universities.[4] Whereas peacetime language teaching had aimed at an appreciation of literature and culture, the military goal was strictly pragmatic: command of the colloquial spoken form of the language in order to communicate directly with natives. Such an aim, which paralleled that of EFL teaching in the United States, brought with it a new methodology.

For each language there was a senior instructor who planned the program, taught the grammar classes, prepared material, supervised the work of the "drill masters," and prepared and administered tests. He did not have to be a native speaker, but needed a knowledge of linguistic analysis. Usually he was a staff member of a university. The drill master, a native speaker of the target language, conducted oral practice sessions and served as a model for the trainee. Prohibited from using English, he was initially to impart correct pronunciation and memorization of the basic sentence patterns.

In practice, there was wide variation among programs in

the number of hours per week. In a survey of German classes, contact hours in individual sections ranged from twelve to twenty-five, with an average of sixteen. The time devoted to general instruction, that is, explanation, varied from zero to eight hours, with an average of five. Drill hours varied from two to twenty-five hours and averaged eleven.[5] More regular was the practice of holding grammar classes for large groups, compared with the drill sections, which were usually fewer than twelve students. The term consisted of a twelve-week period, with one week between terms. The number of terms varied according to the curriculum. The program was divided into two phases: basic and advanced. The basic phase was roughly comparable to the first one and one-half years of college and lasted about three twelve-week terms (nine months), while the advanced phase usually contained up to four terms, which was considered sufficient to bring the student up to the army's required level of competence.

Beginning language habits were established by questions and answers. The teacher gave the question and answer, and the students repeated both. Later the teacher asked the question, and the student provided the answer.[6] The focus of the course was on command of the spoken colloquial language. The point at which orthography was introduced depended on the degree of correspondence between the sound system and the writing system. Following is the development of a course that meets seventeen hours a week:[7]

1. One-hour demonstrations are presented five days a week in pronunciation, grammar, word formation, and so on. Only as much grammar is given as enables the student to generalize in different situations patterns he has already learned by drill and example.

2. There are two-hour drill sessions six days a week with a drill master, preferably native born, in which the material discussed in the demonstration is practiced in the conversation. Not more than ten students are in a drill session.

3. Except for dictation, reading and writing play minimum roles.

4. For drilling, the drill master reads a few questions and answers at normal conversational speed. After two or three readings, the class repeats each sentence in chorus, then individually.

5. A printed copy is distributed and the class reads the text aloud for ten minutes.

6. The class then divides into two groups of five that repeat the questions and answers. Mistakes are corrected by the members.

7. After ten minutes the printed copies are put away. Key words are placed on the blackboard, and the class is divided into five groups of two. Five separate dialogues are then carried on, the instructor going around to listen.

8. Vocabulary is based on everyday needs instead of word frequency lists. Words are learned in short phrases rather than individually. This vocabulary is seldom over fifteen hundred words.

9. The course uses such devices as records, simulated short-wave broadcasts, and lectures by foreign visitors. Meals are served in restaurants where the foreign language is spoken. Students also participate in editing a foreign language newspaper.

10. There is often a periodic rotation of teachers, in order to subject students to a wide variety of speech peculiarities.

Considerable use was made of visual material, in which the objects and actions of the pictures were already known to the students from the oral-aural lesson. Throughout the entire course, subject matter included normal everyday situations as well as information on such subjects as the culture, history, and geography of the area.

Vocabulary was handled in two ways: as part of the build-ups and drills in the regular oral training and as the basis of the lesson, which centered around a particular subject. In the first, the words might derive from several different colloquial situations, while in the second, the entire session was devoted to a single subject, for example, objects in the class, parts of the body, clothing, things to eat and drink, travel, and so forth.

The course featured such practices as a "language table," in which the students ate at tables where only the target language was spoken. Such practice was found most successful when the staff participated and supervised the conversation at the meals. Another technique was the *Comédie Spontanée*, especially for advanced classes. The students were placed in given real-life situations and had to react accordingly. If possible, the situation involved vocabulary drawn from previous lessons. Usually the students questioned the teacher, who played a certain role in the situation. For example, a detachment of paratroopers lands in France with the purpose of cutting German communications lines. The teacher plays the first native they meet, a sympathetic Frenchman who wants to help, and they interrogate him.[8]

In the early stages, need for oral correction was low because of the "mimicry-memorization" approach of completely controlled responses. However, at the more advanced stages, with considerable oral response, the problem of accuracy became greater. Accordingly, the typical ASTP course focused more on fluency in the early stages and on accuracy at the advanced levels.

The amount of reading employed depended on the problems associated with the writing system, and a distinction was made between western European languages and Oriental and eastern European languages. Reading in the second group was introduced one to six weeks after the oral beginning and only in romanized form. With western European languages, reading in normal orthography often began at once and often provided the basis for the conversation exercises. Very simple at first, the material was used for the question-answer drills, which might precede, accompany, or follow the readings.[9] Reading was also used for oral development in the following way:

1. The students read the story at home.

2. Questions and guide words are put on the board in two separate columns: questions about things that happened in the story and key words providing the answers.

3. The student retells part of the story.

4. In a second retelling, the guide words are removed, but the questions remain.

5. In a following retelling, the questions are also removed.[10]

Many instructors found that the oral work helped greatly in the development of reading ability. Robert Hall notes that his ASTP students in Italian were able to read better after three months of intensive study than comparable students would after two years of language taught by a "reading method."[11] A study of W. Freeman Twaddell's ASTP German course at the University of Wisconsin revealed that "the men trained to speak soon reached a point where they surpassed the United States reading norms of men who had spent comparable time solely on learning to read."[12] Writing was not an objective per se but was conceived chiefly as an aid to achieving the main goal. Dictation was the most widely used written exercise. Unfamiliar material was read at a normal pace, and one student wrote on the board immediately after the exercise. Then the students checked their dictation against the board work, which was corrected by the teacher. In general, the ASTP program contained the following features:

1. A large number of class hours in relatively short time
2. Small size of classes
3. Combined presentation of language structure and conversational practice
4. Emphasis on drill and formation of automatic linguistic habits
5. The use of phonemic analysis and transcription
6. The use of native informants
7. The specific goal: command of colloquial speech

Since emphasis was on the colloquial language, existing texts based on the written and literary language were not suitable. The need for a different approach gave rise to new kinds of textbooks, which are best exemplified by some of the EFL texts, especially those published by the University of Michigan.

The ASTP program was carried on by hundreds of language instructors in over fifty colleges and universities. Although the army suggested the general methodology, there was latitude for experiment and innovation within local staffs. Thus, though based on the army's general directives, the

ASTP was "a collection of highly individualized adaptations and experiments as it actually existed in various colleges and universities; the civilian programs developed from it were no less diverse."[13]

The success of the ASTP provoked a flood of articles in magazines such as *Fortune, Reader's Digest, The New York Times Magazine,* and *Science Digest* about the possibilities of its peacetime uses. A voluminous postwar bibliography attests to the interest of the academic community. Of course, conditions were different, and modifications necessary before the ASTP experience could be utilized in regular university teaching. A chief difficulty for peacetime application was fitting into a three-hour course, the usual allotted time, material which required a minimum of ten hours. Some schools were able to make the change. Yale, for example, offered a ten-hour course in French, with seven hours of practice and three hours of explanation. Another problem was the smaller class size necessary for a really effective use of the oral-aural method. College classes of thirty to forty students were clearly too large. In addition, the ASTP had a single utilitarian goal of oral command, while colleges tended to focus on reading knowledge. Charles Hyneman saw the peacetime applications as fourfold: providing new methodology; having a substantial effect on the content of the undergraduate curriculum, especially the culture-area studies aspect of language teaching; providing a program for training Americans who will be working overseas; and supplying a model for the postwar influx of foreign students.[14]

One of the most influential institutions in the field of EFL teaching is the University of Michigan English Language Institute (ELI), which was formed in 1939. In 1940 the institute received a grant from the Rockefeller Foundation to develop materials for an intensive course in English for Latin-American students.[15] From that time it expanded rapidly as various government agencies contributed funds for English teaching to different Latin-American groups.

The first training course for EFL teachers began in the summer of 1942 and included both United States and South American teachers of English.[16] By 1944 the annual enrollment of students learning English reached 236. At this time some of the most influential early volumes in the analysis and teaching of English as a foreign language began to appear. In 1945, Charles Fries published his *Teaching and Learning English as a Foreign Language* and Kenneth Pike contributed *Intonation of American English*. In 1950 the *Intensive Course in English*, begun in 1942 as material for Spanish-speaking students, was revised and published in four separate volumes for pronunciation, grammar, vocabulary, and pattern practice. The present format is the revised edition of 1958. By the end of its first ten years, 1941–50, the ELI had enrolled 2,100 students. In 1953 it produced an examination for a certificate of proficiency in English for the United States Information Agency, a welcome step in establishing overseas evaluation of English proficiency.

In 1956, Fries retired from the ELI after directing the program for fifteen years. During this time the institute's regular course consisted of eight-week intensive sessions; not until 1963 was a fifteen-week intensive course offered in addition.[17] The intensive course, its methodology and materials, was developed under the guiding hand of Fries, whose main approach is outlined in *Teaching and Learning English as a Foreign*

Language. He stresses that in learning a new language, the most important initial step is not acquisition of vocabulary but mastering the sound system:* "to understand the stream of speech, to hear distinctive sound features and to approximate their production."[19] After that come the elements which compose the structure of the language: morphology and syntax. There must only be sufficient vocabulary to operate the structures and convey the sound system actually used. No matter what the ultimate goal, language learning must be developed through oral practice. Even if the student is interested only in reading, "the mastery of the fundamentals of the language . . . the structure and sound system with a limited vocabulary . . . must be through speech."[20]

In discussing the need for a realistic grammar of English, Fries insists that such an analysis contain "an accurate description of the structural system . . . of the devices used and the way they operate together to express the necessary structural meanings."[21] He attempts to provide this analysis in a later volume, *The Structure of English.* From such an ideal grammar, the EFL text or syllabus must select and arrange sequentially the basic patterns necessary for learning in a controlled situation. The author suggests range of usefulness and regularity of form as the criteria for choosing patterns for the introductory course.

Fries rejects the Gouin concept of language learning as imitating the process of the child. In learning material, it is neither desirable nor feasible for a student to repeat the learning process of the child, who is exposed to a farrago of patterns and only slowly develops mastery over them through

* Fries was the first, since Sapir enunciated it in 1925, to use the concept of sound patterns for a practical pedagogical purpose.[18]

years of trial and error practice. Instead, the adult learner acquires one pattern at a time through a series of controlled exercises and is thus able to reduce the wasteful number of mistakes that children invariably make. These controlled structural exercises should have semantic relevance to the student's environment to avoid artificiality. Moreover, students tend to retain contextual material far better than isolated sentences.

Regarding the place of words and the concept of meaning, Fries suggests that there are at least four important levels of meaning in English:

1. *Lexical meaning*—the meaning of words as listed in the dictionary.

2. *Syntactic meaning*—word order; words acquire added meaning by relation to other words in a sentence.

3. *Morphological meaning*—the forms of words; the meaning that derives from such changes as *foot* to *feet* or *give* to *gave*.

4. *Stress*; the way a word is pronounced can change its meaning considerably.[22]

Very few words have only one meaning; in fact, most have fifteen to twenty, and it is almost impossible for a word in two different languages to have the same meaning in all, or even most, different contexts. Thus, in teaching vocabulary, the only true meanings of words are the specific contexts they appear in.

Finding no EFL texts based even on the meager existing descriptive analyses of English, the ELI set about developing its own material. Following Fries's guidelines, the material is always introduced orally, and statements on structure "are always summaries or generalizations drawn from the actual sentences the students have already practiced."[23] Since in English there is a far poorer correlation between sounds and letters than in Spanish or Finnish, for example, the material employs a modified phonemic alphabet.

In its present form, the *Intensive Course in English* contains four volumes: *English Sentence Patterns, English Pattern Practice, English Pronunciation,* and *Lessons in Vocabulary.* In all four, with notable exceptions in *Lessons in Vocabulary,* there is little in the way of "contextual material." Sentences chosen for exercises are perfectly normal utterances, but they seldom have any relation to one another. This is one of the greatest drawbacks in the intensive course. In addition, almost all responses are completely controlled, and there is little provision for students to generate any utterances different from the controlled responses being practiced. Since the student may not yet be ready to contribute original thoughts, these two problems are not too serious at the beginning level, where a high degree of control is necessary in order to inculcate habits and prevent too many mistakes. However, by the intermediate and advanced levels the text must contain formal provisions for eliciting the student's own utterances in a range of increasing semantic freedom. Such provisions at the intermediate and advanced levels are even now only starting to appear in books like Jean Praninskas' *Rapid Review of English Grammar.*

The methodology of the intensive course materials, which were originally designed for Spanish-speaking students, was adopted *in toto* by EFL programs in other institutions and came to be used for all foreign students. Kenneth Croft estimates that the Michigan "technology" underlies more than half the EFL texts published in the United States in the last twenty years and a great many EFL texts published overseas.[24] The Michigan method is often equated with the ASTP approach, but there are definite differences between the two. The ELI materials were highly organized from the grammatical point of view. They were carefully divided into pronunciation, structure, vocabulary, and pattern practice, with pattern practice as the primary feature of the program. The ASTP, on the other hand, used a mimicry-memorization technique by which students memorized dialogues from everyday situations. They then did exercises based on the dialogues, with no appreciable use of pattern practice. The program was not characterized by careful grammatical arrangement but was situation oriented. While both used an essentially phonemic approach, Michigan did not neglect phonetic correction, particularly pronunciation. In addition, it taught each sound in isolation as well as in combined form,[25] while the ASTP, because of its own particular goals, placed far lighter emphasis on pronunciation. The ASTP methodology, according to Croft, had a much smaller influence on EFL texts produced in the United States, about 10 per cent, but had a greater effect on texts produced overseas.[26] "The major role played by the Michigan and ASTP technologies has been in the area of basic courses, those designed for beginning-level and low intermediate-level students."[27]

Inherent in the ELI materials is Fries's descriptive grammar of English, which is presented in his volume *The Structure of English*. The book attempts to provide a new picture of the English language based chiefly on the analysis of actual recorded conversations, and is devoted almost completely to syntax. The author rejects the traditional parts of speech and divides the language into four major form classes and a category of function words containing fifteen subgroups. These function words, says Gleason, "are not the structure of the sentence; they are only the signals of that structure."[28] According to Fries, a function word "has little or no meaning apart from the grammatical idea it expresses."[29] Sentences contain two kinds of meaning: lexical meaning, the dictionary meaning of words in isolation; and structural meaning, signal words that indicate the relationship of words in the sentence and express such things as time—past, present—and number—singular, plural. "The grammar of a language consists of the devices that signal structural meaning."[30]

Structural grammar was considerably influenced by descriptive linguistics, "particularly the Bloomfieldian point of view of the 1930's and 1940's."[31] Although it had an extremely mixed reception among grammarians, linguists, and English teachers, it has exerted considerable influence on those whose professions deal with the English language.

Another institution instrumental in EFL development in the early 1940's was Wilson's Teacher's College. Financed by the State Department, the National Education Association, and the United States Office of Education, it handled thousands of students and offered a proving ground for courses, methods, teachers, and standards of student achievement.

The teachers were mostly those with Latin-American experience in EFL, with a minimum of five years in teaching. Begun in 1942, the program was organized on a continuous rather than a term basis, so that students could enter and leave at virtually any time. This fitted in particularly well with many students who were not tied to the academic year.

The program itself contained five levels of English: beginning, low intermediate, high intermediate, low advanced, and high advanced. Students were given separate auditory comprehension, grammar, and reading tests for placement. Many foreign students have an extremely large reading vocabulary but still have great trouble in speaking and understanding. A student in this category often entered a low class for a short period of time but was promoted "as rapidly as his ears begin to understand the words his eyes already know."[32] Classes were limited to ten students, each teacher having at his disposal the school's complete resources of texts, visual aids, and other materials. The teacher was free to select and use them in any way he felt best fitted the needs of the group. The two lowest levels used the following volumes:

1. I. A. Richards, *The Pocket Book of Basic English* (New York, Pocket Books, 1948).

2. Orthological Institute, *Learning the English Language— A Book for Men and Women of All Countries* (Boston, Houghton Mifflin, 1943). Books I, II and III use the basic vocabulary from Richards but develop it in greater detail.

3. I. A. Richards, *Anglophone Pocket Book Course in Basic English* (Washington, Educational Services, 1949), an album of records correlated with item one. Students repeat recorded statements which allow time for repetition.

4. Film strips, obtained from Harvard University, related to the records and the *Pocket Book*. The film strips were also used simultaneously with the records for ear training.

5. Volumes One and Two of the *Intensive Course in English*, from the English Language Institute, University of Michigan.

6. Newspapers, starting with the low intermediate level.

The three highest levels used:

7. Volumes Three and Four of the *Intensive Course in English*, University of Michigan.
8. Material for auditory training: the teacher reads a passage; he then explains unfamiliar words, idioms, and phrases, and writes them on the blackboard; he rereads the passage, several times if necessary, breaking up the sentences into phrases and having the students repeat; he renders a final reading, after which the students retell the story or write down their recollection of it.

Students are taught the phonemic symbols and are given frequent drills on sound discrimination, practicing minimal pairs, and other materials. One period a day is also devoted to American civilization, usually in the form of film strips which are presented in the following manner: the teacher obtains the script, simplifies the structures, but retains the lexicon of the film; the film is run twice (the best length for a film is about ten minutes); afterward, during a regular period, the class discusses the film or is asked to answer certain questions in writing; occasionally, written questions about the film are used as a test.[33]

In order to strengthen vocabulary, engineering students began to audit science classes as soon as their English was considered proficient enough. In addition, the center held vocabulary classes for one hour three times a week for special disciplines, such as medicine.

Though not involved in EFL, Pierre Delattre embodies the most advanced concepts in foreign-language teaching during the late 1930's and 1940's. His work is valuable both historically and as an aid to dealing with certain current problems.

From 1938–44, Delattre published fifteen to twenty articles on research in applied and experimental phonetics and was responsible for the early scientific, structurally controlled use of the oral-aural method.

Delattre urged the temporary elimination of writing while the essential meaning-sound associations are being made. To this end, he utilized the phonograph, which "can do what the professor hasn't time to do. It can create in the student automatic reactions. It can repeat without fatigue or varying."[34] Delattre evolved a course in which the text is replaced entirely by records in the early stages. The results, he remarks, are excellent. The students enjoy the new approach and spend more time with their lessons than they did when textbooks were used. The records include the new text, plus questions and exercises about it.

Further justifying his emphasis on the sound system, Delattre explains that the student who studies the sounds exclusively can focus his attention on accuracy, position of the vocal organs, intonation, and other features of phrase and word. Graphic, or alphabetic, symbols in the target language are invariably associated with those in the mother tongue. This association causes automatic articulatory movement toward previously known sounds. Thus, instead of the exact sounds of the target language, there is invariably a modification of the mother tongue. Delattre states that in language teaching we do not make sufficient use of the sound memory, which is the mechanism by which we learn the first language. He emphasizes that words represent sounds, *"et nous persistone à les apprendre par des signes. Ce procédé indirect affaiblit et peut-être même déforme la mémoire sonore."*[35] He affirms that grammar is useful as a means of extending to a growing number of cases the characteristics observed in a few cases.

Before students use the record, the lesson is prepared in class with the teacher. The student then practices between classes in order to develop a more automatic response. On the records Delattre uses techniques of gradually adding words to an original core or phrase—graduated additions— and substituting different form classes. He suggests that addition and substitution exercises are excellent for forming intonation habits, in contrast to the ASTP, which often sacrifices quality for rapidity.[36]

A sixteen-week semester contains twenty units of recorded material learned in a completely oral manner during the first thirteen weeks. The last three weeks are then spent on spelling of the twenty units and practice of reading and writing.[37] The three first lessons include just one basic sentence per week, composed of twenty words. All questions are phrased so that the answers are drawn from the material in sentences, such as the following:

Week 1: La belle demoiselle qui passe là-bas est la voisine de Jeanne à la classe de mathématique de la capitale.

Week 2: Le jeune monsieur qui travaille à côté est le nouveau professeur de Charlot au cours de littérature espagnole du Collège.

Week 3: Le gentil garçon qui prononce bien a un voisin ennuyeux qui bavarde constamment dans une classe de français à Verdun.

Sentence one, week one, contains no *r* sound, no rounded vowels or nasal vowels, and presents only four open vowels and / ∂ /. Sentence two has no nasal vowels but is devoted to rounded vowels and introduction of *r*. Sentence three focuses on nasal vowels.

Unit One, which provides for five days the first week, is built around basic sentence one in the following way. In the first class period, two-thirds of the hour is devoted to "covering features," such as intonation and translation of the words; rhythm; stress; and syllabification. The rest of the hour is spent in giving physiological directives for vowels, fronting; for consonants, fronting of alveolars, *détente* of finals, non-aspiration of voiceless stops; for vowels and consonants, tension.

Day 1. The first assignment is to memorize the basic sentence, using the records, which give the sentence in echelon pattern. The sentence is gradually built up, piece by piece, with time given for repetition after each echelon. The echelons are repeated once for each covering feature.

Day 2. Students give individual recitations of echelons. A good deal of correction is necessary. Dozens of questions and substitution patterns are prepared. The answers utilize only the words of the basic sentence. The second assignment consists of intensive practice of the first set of questions, using the record with blanks left for answers. In addition, the students must perfect the basic sentence by further studying the first record.

Day 3. Questions are easily answered, but phonetic correction is still needed. Students recite the basic sentence again. Two new sets of questions are introduced, to be answered only with words from the basic sentence.

Day 4. By this time, the students have acquired better pronunciation of the answers and the basic sentences. Three new sets of questions are introduced, using the same words.

Day 5. There is a review of the answers and the basic sentence. The assignment is to review all of the questions.

Unit Two, week two, is introduced by substitutions, starting with sentence one and changing one word or group of words at a time until basic sentence two finally emerges. The sentence is practiced in echelon, giving a second opportunity to go over the covering features. The first assignment is to memorize the substitution sentences and echelon sentences. The remainder of the unit is similar to Unit One, with four days of questions, increasing in amount each day.

Unit Three, week three, like Unit Two, is introduced by substitutions which gradually produce basic sentence three. Phonetic directions are given each time a nasal vowel is introduced by substitution. The sentence is practiced in echelon as in the previous two units. The first assignment involves substitutions and echelons; the second, third, and fourth are devoted to substitutions and questions and answers graded in echelons; the fifth assignment contains a review of all three units.

Thus the focus in the first three units is on pronunciation. After this foundation, a new phase begins in which vocabulary is continually increased. The seventeen units covered in the next ten weeks all use records and follow the same approach as before. There is varied material in the statements to be memorized and abundant questions covering all the words in the statement. In the records, statements are followed by pauses for repeating; questions are followed by pauses for answering. Lessons four through twenty alternate between structure-centered and subject-centered lessons. For example, Lesson 11 deals with reflexive verbs of human action, while Lesson 12 deals with the family.

Four oral tests are given during the first semester, one every four weeks. Each of the first three sets, a maximum of ten minutes each, are a conversation with the teacher. The last test is fifteen minutes in length. The final two-hour examination is written and is based on the spelling work of the last three weeks in the series. Lexicon, grammar, and dictation sentences for translation are included.

Delattre remarks that although the students in his test group had been writing for only a few weeks, their grammar compared favorably with a book-centered class that he was using as a control group.[38] The second semester followed the more common use of reading, grammar, and composition. However, Delattre was able to use a considerable amount of French in discussions and explanations. There was a continued but more limited use of records. While praising the work of Fries, Delattre suggested that the Michigan method introduced the written word too early from the point of view of establishing psychological and physiological habits.[39]

The teaching of EFL had long been neglected in the United States prior to World War II. Work had been done for immigrants and other groups, but conditions were poor, and teachers were undertrained, underpaid, and overworked. This situation began to change shortly before the war as United States advances in technology brought many foreigners to work and study in American universities, hospitals, social agencies, and government bureaus. With the war, the closing of universities in Europe and the training programs for Allied military personnel greatly increased the numbers who needed to learn English.[40]

These students were without the handicaps of advanced age or inferior educational, social, or economic status, like many of the earlier immigrants. Instead of being isolated, they were part of agencies and institutions with trained personnel and other facilities far beyond those previously devoted to EFL. Skilled language teachers and linguists found this new type of foreign student on their own campuses and were called in to help.[41] The result was a degree of interest and experimentation approaching that of the ASTP.

Actually, the military program was not the only force for rejuvenating language teaching. In the Southwest an increase in the Spanish-speaking population began to present a communication problem for several states. Spanish and EFL came to be taught in the elementary schools. And this EFL teaching at lower levels resulted in experiments with new methods and materials. "The tide of foreigners seeking to learn English here or in their own country was rising ever higher," and the teaching of EFL began "to come into its own after being treated as a stepchild for many years."[42]

In 1911 there were only 3,645 foreign students in American institutions of higher learning.[43] Gradually the number rose, reaching 6,488 in 1921,[44] 9,961 in 1930, and 10,341 in 1945 after a sharp drop during the depression.[45] After the war the figures began to mount steeply. By 1946 they jumped to over 16,176, with 26,433 by 1949 and 34,200 in 1954. By 1961 enrollment of foreign students reached 53,107 and then soared to 82,000 in 1964.[46] If current projections continue, there will be 100,000 foreign students in American colleges and universities by 1970.[47] Who are these foreign students? Why are they here? What role does EFL play in their total experience of a new culture?

Cora DuBois observed certain quantitative changes in the foreign student population between 1930 and 1953. The year 1930 was chosen as representative, since it was the last year before the effects of the depression began to be felt. During this period the United States college student population rose 100 per cent, while foreign student enrollment increased 300 per cent. Moreover, foreign students began to be found in a greater number of institutions. This dispersal created a problem for small colleges that had a limited number of foreign students but not enough to warrant the development of an EFL program. Another change was the relative and absolute increase in students from countries with cultures considerably different from American culture. During the period the proportion of students from South America, the Middle East, and South Asia rose more than 300 per cent.[48] From 1953 to 1963, Africans from south of the Sahara increased about 300 per cent and those from Asia even more.

Another trend is toward greater numbers of graduate students. In 1964–65, 43 per cent of foreign students were graduates and 46 per cent undergraduates, with 11 per cent unspecified. In 1963–64, 42 per cent were graduates, 48 per cent undergraduates, and 10 per cent unspecified, while in 1954 only 36 per cent were graduates, 58 per cent undergraduates, and 6 per cent unspecified.[49] This trend reflects an attitude of more and more American colleges encouraging foreign students to prepare as much as they can in their own countries before coming to the United States. It also reflects the growth of undergraduate institutions in foreign countries.[50] The greater maturity of foreign students must be reflected in increasingly sophisticated semantic content of EFL materials. Many of these students will be doctors, scientists, and businessmen. Selections like "A Day with the Johnson Family" are an insult to their intelligence.[51]

"The international commitments of the American college and university are permanent; they are not merely here to stay, but to increase. This means that they can no longer be dealt with on an *ad hoc* basis."[52] These commitments have three valid justifications: the self-interests of the university, the national interest of the United States, and the interest of the international community.[53] In all these areas the role of the foreign student is central. First of all, by his curricular and extracurricular contributions the foreign student adds to the international understanding of fellow students and faculty. Secondly, the government's entire foreign exchange program is based on the proposition that those who spend several years studying in the United States will be favorably impressed by American institutions and will reflect this good will after returning to their own countries. Finally, the international community clearly is well served by an ever widening communication of ideas between nations, centers of learning, and individuals.

Another important element is the level of English competence required for admission to colleges in contrast to the foreign student's actual language preparation. In a 1952 survey of 257 foreign students, Cieslak reports that under half (47 per cent) had to submit evidence of English proficiency prior to admission.[54] Most frequently the evidence of proficiency consisted of statements by consular officials, cultural attachés, English teachers overseas, or an officer from a school the student attended. The second most used evidence was a statement that English had been studied in secondary school. Twenty-three per cent of the foreign students surveyed listed screening of English by individuals who had returned home from the United States. Thirty-five per cent stated that no proficiency in English was required. Such means of evaluation are especially dangerous if we accept Cieslak's estimate that of the students who have had previous English instruction little more than half have had training in conversation. On the basis of the 122 schools that replied to his questionnaire, Cieslak observes that about half the foreign students in United States colleges seem to need remedial English and that only 59 per cent of those institutions queried provided English courses different from those for American students.[55]

A questionnaire circulated by the Association of Graduate Schools and the Association of American Universities in 1953 showed that of the thirty-four universities replying, twenty-one gave no English examination to foreign students either before or upon entrance to graduate school. Nine gave examinations to all entering foreign students; four gave examinations only to those referred by departments or advisers. The survey data suggest that about half the members of the associations regarded "the English ability of the students as a problem requiring attention."[56] A study made by the Committee on Educational Interchange Policy found that about one-third of the 58,000 foreign students in American institutions in 1962 were thoroughly screened to make sure they had the necessary financial support, academic preparation, and language proficiency. Another third were partially screened, and the final third had no screening at all. One- to two-thirds of the foreign students coming to the United States were in some degree deficient in financial resources and academic preparation, including knowledge of English.[57] Estimates were that as high as 40 per cent of the 58,000 had inadequate preparation in English. For some areas the number was close to 100 per cent, especially from French-speaking North Africa, Morocco and Tunisia, and from Southeast Asia, that is, those countries with the greatest need to send students abroad for training. In many of these countries, where English is neither a first nor a second language and where language teaching still uses antiquated methods, the situation is not likely to improve in the immediate future.

The degree of English competence required varies among different institutions. The possibilities include:

1. *A highly restrictive standard*—admitting only those who have no further need of English-language training.

2. *A flexible standard*—encouraging those who have an English-language deficiency but who meet the other academic qualifications. Students are then required to take EFL training at the school.

3. *A moderate standard*—admitting students whose competence in English, on the basis of overseas credentials, is presumed adequate for academic needs but who will be able to take language work if it is needed.[58]

For most universities, a highly restricted standard is impractical. In addition, relatively few institutions are able to present a full EFL program designed to accommodate students who have an English language deficiency. However, there are several possible solutions to the problem:

1. Developing regional EFL centers throughout the country.

2. Requiring students to attend an integrated EFL program somewhere in the United States before beginning their academic studies.*

3. Requiring additional EFL training in the home country.

In practice all three solutions are being used. Several groups of small colleges have already joined together to establish language teaching centers in mutually accessible areas.[60] However, the last alternative seems the most practical in terms of the foreign student and his sponsor, as it is far less expensive for the student to study English at a language center in his own country than to spend one or two semesters studying it in the United States before going on to regular academic studies. In conjunction with this, USIS and other United States overseas programs in EFL can provide invaluable service by offering courses and administering proficiency tests.

As a way of ensuring proper English preparation for proposed studies, DuBois suggests the use of standardized tests that could be administered by cultural officers and consular officials overseas.[61] Present evaluations based on statements of teachers or conversations with officials or former students are highly variable and are often of little value. An evaluation based on a standardized test would give the student a more realistic picture for his own proposed course of study. Actually, there has been considerable progress in this area, as evidenced by the Michigan test and a newer one designed by the Educational Testing Service, Princeton, New Jersey.

Why is the foreign student here, and how does language

---

* It is interesting that the Soviet Union provides a year of intensive language instruction to students from Asia and Africa before sending them on for further studies.[59]

ability affect his aims and the totality of his new experience?
A study of several hundred random applications made to the
Institute of International Education (IIE) by students from
a number of countries reveals the following goals in order
of importance:

1. To advance the student's personal and professional development

2. To prepare the student for service to his country through
acquisition of additional knowledge and skills

3. To promote international understanding

4. To contribute to the advancement of knowledge through
co-operative study and research with professional colleagues
in the United States[62]

How does language proficiency affect students' academic
performance? Mestenhauser lists several studies, all of which
show "a high positive correlation between high scores on objective language tests and satisfactory or better grade averages"
and an "equally strong correlation between low test scores
and academic failure."[63] According to Mestenhauser, the
causes of academic failure include the following:

1. Inadequate academic preparation in the home country

2. The United States examination system (second most important cause). Students must adapt to new and different patterns of study, learning, and reasoning. It may be possible
for the EFL program, utilizing cultural materials in the
course, to provide an introductory experience to the new
system.

3. The psychological effect of being a foreign student and
being inadequate to meet demands such as participating ac-

tively in class before being psychologically or linguistically prepared to do so. In this context, the EFL class can provide an ideal proving ground, where the student can participate in discussion and present talks of his own under an instructor's supervision.

What significance does the EFL factor have in personal adjustment? Cora DuBois, a psychiatrist who has done considerable work with foreign students, believes that "the importance of the interpersonal relations as well as the importance of the whole formal education process will be mediated by the ability to communicate. Language therefore, is a factor of primary importance in the sojourn adjustment."[64] That the foreign student is aware of this EFL factor was revealed by an IIE questionnaire issued in 1952. Of the 1,042 Department of State grantees who replied, 30 per cent were from English-speaking countries and had no difficulty; 16 per cent had no difficulty although they were from non-English-speaking countries; but 51 per cent noted that they had difficulty with the language. The majority, 47 per cent, had trouble understanding others, while 25 per cent had trouble in speaking. The high figure of 47 per cent suggests possible need for greater work in auditory comprehension, a need that could be dealt with most economically in the language laboratory. DuBois further states:

> The degree of command of English which a foreign student brings with him and acquires during his sojourn is . . . one of his most significant skills, and at the same time a symptom of his capacity to understand and deal with the American environment, particularly the highly verbalizing environment of colleges and universities. A low ability in . . . English is a

serious handicap. . . . It may serve to isolate the student from supportive American contacts on both personal and academic levels. It greatly increases the educational strain, and may reduce the chances of goal achievements that are so necessary to satisfactory adjustment. For, in a large degree, the labor required by a student to perform adequately in his studies is a function of his mastery of the language.[65]

A study made in 1960 by Richard Morris showed that the range of contact with Americans was appreciably lower among students with language difficulty than among those without it. The language barrier made it harder to explore the new culture to any extent. The study further revealed that "those with language difficulty are restrained in contact . . . that students who cannot use English with facility in maintaining relations with Americans find the strain of talking across language barriers too great."[66]

VI

Principles and Methods: Linguistic Theory and Language Teaching

UNTIL RECENTLY, most EFL programs followed the Michigan approach and to a lesser extent the ASTP. The chief limitations in the Michigan method are lack of provisions for eliciting original responses and lack of contextual material. There has been increasing awareness of the need for presenting material in a contextual situation rather than in isolation. The idea of context can be viewed in two ways. First, the material in any area—pronunciation, vocabulary, syntax—is presented in units larger than the word or the sentence; that is, the lexicon, pattern, or item of pronunciation is contained in material of paragraph length. Second, this idea can be followed even in pattern practice; responses containing the item being learned are drawn from the student's own background. In this way, the context is provided by the student's own internal environment, his own personal system of recollections and associations. The idea of context, plus another major concept of moving from the mechanical to the communicative production of sentences, will be examined in the section on syntax.

Most foreign-language programs seem to recognize a need

for different levels of competence, which are somewhat arbitrarily designated as elementary, intermediate, and advanced. The elementary level, suggests Nelson Brooks, should contain all of the phonology, the most important syntactic patterns used in talking, and a large number of the most frequent morphological items. In addition, it should present most of the structure words and a modest number of vocabulary items.[1] Fries's outline is similar,[2] as is Mary Finocchiaro's, except that she recommends a more even distribution of grammatical patterns among the three levels.[3] The areas of the intermediate and advanced course are harder to delineate and will be explored in the section on syntax. The language elements that should be selected for teaching are those the language is least able to do without in functioning as an effective means of communication. Mackey uses the term *restrictability*; the more restrictable an item is in its occurrence, the less need there is for teaching it. Conversely, the less restricted, the more widespread an item, the greater its importance in the language. It is very difficult to restrict occurrences of most phonemes, for example, without altering the language system itself.[4] Furthermore, the lower the level of the course, the less free choice there is in what items to include. At the beginning level, items such as phonology, articles, and many structure words are essential to meaningful expression in the language. With most of the widespread necessary elements covered at the elementary level, the more advanced levels allow greater freedom in the choice of material.

One of the more talked-about concepts in modern foreign language teaching is programmed instruction, whose principles are summed up by John B. Carroll:

1. Progress must be based on an adequately detailed terminal behavior, that is, the skills the student is supposed to have acquired by the end of the program.

2. The material must be presented in a specific sequence of steps which enable the student to move gradually from simpler to more difficult items. Here transformational grammar can be used to separate sentences that contain differences in deep structure.

3. Provisions must be made for the student to test the mastery of each step and correct it if it is wrong.[5]

To date, there are no programmed EFL texts that are available. "Even when such programmed texts do become widely available," suggests Clifford Prator, "there is no reason to believe that they will bring a radical methodological breakthrough in language teaching. Actually, all the essential features of programmed instruction have for a decade or more, been part of the linguistically oriented classes which are common in the field of English as a Second Language."[6]

Ferdinand Marty emphasizes that material should be introduced in small amounts over several weeks rather than in a single, massed presentation. He has found that automatic responses are better acquired if the time allocated is broken up into small blocks. He conducted experiments with two groups of students learning French. In learning the pattern *He would have succeeded if he had worked*, students practiced changing the tense from present conditional/past indicative, *He would succeed if he worked*, to the past conditional/pluperfect, *He would have succeeded if he had worked*. The first group (group A) studied one hour and achieved automatic responses, while the second group (group B) practiced twenty minutes and achieved a correct but halting response. After another twenty-minute session on the second day with both groups, there was no difference between the two and there had been a waste of forty minutes with group A.[7] The same principle obtains with vocabulary. Practicing a word ten or twenty times in one hour is not as useful as a large number of single uses at regular intervals. Moreover, a cyclical review of the structures and vocabulary must be included in each lesson.

Marty defines programming as "the process of organizing the material to be learned in such a way that the subject acquires the linguistic behavior with maximum efficiency."[8] In most university programs the criterion chosen is usually one of time. Marty makes several obvious and some not-so-obvious suggestions for laying out the foreign language course:

1. The programmer should have a complete description of the linguistic behavior he intends to teach. This includes the language structures, morphological items, vocabulary, spelling rules, and cultural information.

2. There should be a separate description of the spoken and written forms of the language. The audio form should be presented first, and the written form as soon as oral mastery is acquired. In one of his many language learning experiments conducted over the last decade, Marty found that the time lag between oral and written forms need not be long. In fact, with too long a wait the student cannot keep from visualizing the word in his mind, thus invariably establishing some wrong spellings.

3. After about 150 hours, "crystallization" starts to occur, a process in which the student has assimilated all the structures,

morphology, and lexicon and, using analogy as a guide, is able to generate sentences he has not heard before. Marty warns, however, that uncontrolled analogy can destroy a program as well as guide it to success unless irregular forms—lexical, morphological or syntactic—are sufficiently practiced.

4. For teaching vocabulary, Marty suggests that using only one fixed approach is inadequate and that each new item requires one or several of many different approaches that will fix the item most firmly in the student's mind.

5. He makes a strong plea for cyclical review. "As all programmers know, retention is our greatest problem." Halfway through a program, the student should be spending over 80 per cent of the time on retention frames, the figure rising even higher toward the end of the program.[9]

The teaching of pronunciation has continued to follow the approach of the Michigan school, which emphasizes such concepts as minimal pairs, pitch, stress, and juncture. Michigan also uses the Bloch-Trager-Smith phonemic system of vowels, which reduced the number of English vowels to eight, arranged in three rows and three columns, except for the top central position to which / ɨ / was later added.[10] Prior to this, phonemics followed the vowel pattern of the IPA, the International Phonetic Alphabet, with thirteen vowels arranged symmetrically.

Research by Agard and Dunkel has shown that short utterances of ten to twelve syllables can be imitated by students almost perfectly.[11] However, because students are seldom given enough time for sufficient drill, they tend to relapse into old phonetic patterns. The tendency to revert to old pronunciation patterns increases sharply when the utterance is long or otherwise difficult.

When pronunciation is taught, the classroom should be reserved for explanation and control and the language laboratory used for drill on the material presented previously by the teacher. The complete phonetic lesson should include a presentation of the sound or general features to be drilled, identification of the sound or feature, production and correction, and fixation.[12] Once a mistake has been pointed out, it should be indicated each time it comes up. However, the teacher should not spend too much time drilling the same phonetic problem, as it is far better to distribute the same material over a wider period of time. The phonetics class should start with a review of the previous lesson. The teacher sees that all the students can produce the sound or make the necessary distinction. Repeating contrasting sounds together in class frees the student from self-consciousness; moreover, calling on individuals wastes a great amount of overall class time. The trained teacher will be able to spot mistakes easily enough. For maximum retention, vowels and consonants should be drilled not only in minimal pairs and sentences but, as we have seen, in larger utterances.

The hardest skill to acquire is listening comprehension, which is poorly understood. Léon suggests that initial perception comes through on the syntactic level, that "our students will be able to hear correctly . . . only when they will have mastered all structures of the language! It could be said that we can hear if we already know what is likely to be said."[13] One way out of this dilemma is to teach listening comprehension by first training the students to understand complete sentences or at least groups of words, and then by using minimal pairs in order to train their ears to perceive important acoustical cues.

Imitating sentences without an explanation of meaning (of structural forms, vocabulary, or sound components) makes a presentation far less effective. Though children learn the language this way, they have thousands of hours per year; students usually have about three hundred hours, including class time and homework. Thus, adults must be allowed to use certain mature abilities that children lack. Marty observes that students who do not know the meaningful features of sentences are liable to make small sound changes that cause a shift in meaning.[14]

The basic pronunciation problems should be taken care of at the elementary level, with the necessary refinements made, ideally, by the end of the intermediate stage. The pronunciation problems of the advanced student are extremely difficult to correct, for by this time they have become strongly entrenched and require a disproportionate amount of time. "Trying to improve his pronunciation is strictly uphill work," suggests Praninskas, "and probably not worth the effort in most cases."[15]

In an effort to establish the meaning of foreign words, teachers have used many approaches. Robert Lado suggests the following:

1. Self-defining lexical contexts
2. Definitions
3. Opposites (if one word is already known)
4. Synonyms
5. Dramatizations—acting out meanings

6. Pictures
7. Real objects[16]

But unless this approach presents a full range of meanings, it can lead to a major problem. The word in the foreign language, English, can become equated with one in the student's native language from association in just one context. The foreign word is then used in other contexts where the native word appears. Robert Politzer gives the following examples. In the sentences "I *got* the book from my friend" and "I *received* the book from my friend," *got* is equated with *received*. This association can produce a meaningless sentence like "I *received* excited."[17] By way of further illustration, we can divide the meanings of *get* into sets by the following syntactic structures:

get going	get it going	verb + gerund
get to go	get it to go	verb + to + verb
get married	get it repaired	verb + past participle
get something		verb + noun

It is necessary to present a word in a range of its major semantic environments. Only in this way will the student be prevented from developing a fixed association between one word and one meaning. Often it is not possible to grasp other meanings by context or analogy, and the student is left utterly baffled by a word he thought he knew. A case in point is the word *over*, which has at least the following range of meanings:

1. It happens over and over. (again and again)
2. It's over. (finished)
3. It's over there. (direction)
4. The plane is over New York. (above)

5. It was over the radio.
6. He came over yesterday.
7. It hung over the edge.

Some attempts have been made to collect such words and present illustrative examples of their various meanings,* but far too little has been done to date. The problem of semantic selection is most important at the beginning level, for the most common lexical items also have the most meanings as well, and it is necessary to decide which meanings of a word should be taught at a particular time.[18]

One of the chief areas of investigation in vocabulary teaching is the concept of greater "contextuality" of material. This area has two centers. The first, already discussed, involves the range of meanings of words. The second is to be found at the more advanced levels of language learning, where the lexical needs of the student far outstrip the class time available for teaching individual items. Furthermore, it becomes increasingly important for the student to be able to learn from contexts. This is especially true for reading, where it is virtually impossible to teach a great number of low-frequency words as individual items. A typical frequency distribution is less like a bell-shaped curve than a ski jump and includes a very few very-high-frequency words, a small number of medium-frequency words, and a very large number of very-low-frequency words.[19] In an analysis of his volume *Computational Analyses of Present Day American English*, Francis observes that the ten most frequent words (*the, of, and, to, a, in, that, is, was, he*) account for about one-quarter of the book's one

* One helpful collection is the little volume by Thomas Lee Crowell, Jr., *A Glossary of Phrases with Prepositions.*

million words. The most common single word, *the*, occurs about 70,000 times (once every 15 words). The tenth most frequent, *he*, occurs once in every 106 words. The fiftieth word, *if*, once in every 461. The one hundredth, *down*, once in 1,133.[20] Thus, even near the top of the list there is a very sharp drop. Accordingly, Twaddell concludes that the "intermediate student will not have adequate vocabulary resources until after many many hours of conversation and many hundreds of pages of reading. The resources are scanty; they must be compensated for by skills."[21] These skills involve ascertaining the meaning of an unknown word by its sentence context.

At the elementary level, lexicon is strictly controlled and the student receives many calculated occurrences; thus, interference is kept to a minimum. But at the intermediate level, controls are reduced as the use of language moves closer to a real-life situation and the skill of educated guessing becomes a major aim of teaching. The formal aspects of this skill are best derived from a command of the language structures which clearly indicate that a word is a noun, a verb, or whatever. This ability to discern structural slots (tagmemes) will be discussed in the following section.

The average foreign student coming to the United States does not have an English vocabulary much over 2,000 words.[22] With cognates, the figure may be as high as 5,000. However, any mature prose contains a great number of words well beyond that range. Every adult speaker of a language uses at least 20,000 to 30,000 words; if he is educated and uses technical or learned words, he knows many more.[23] Thus, the student needs at least another 5,000 to be able to read with any degree of ease and speed, and another 15,000 to feel at home in conversation. Furthermore, a larger vocabulary is used in reading than in speaking.[24] Thus, the problems lie in the words of 5,000 to 20,000 frequency because of their limited appearance. In addition to other approaches, lessons might include classified word lists grouped by subjects, which could be drilled and reviewed as single units.

Mackey suggests that the order of introducing concrete nouns should depend on their use in helping clarify grammatical sequences, while the chief criterion for abstract nouns is whether the higher abstractions are based on lower ones which in turn are based on lower ones that define them. Several pages after presenting the words *oranges, apples,* and *lemons,* a text might introduce the word *fruit,* which later combines with *bread, milk,* and *meat* to produce the word *food.* Sequencing of verbs can be arranged according to "actions through which the greatest number of objects can be manipulated. . . . Even highly useful verbs like *see,* which simply express sensation, are not as easy to demonstrate as verbs like *give* and *get,* which can be expressed in the moving of physical objects."[25]

Michael West's *General Service List,* based on the Thorndike-Lorge semantic count, indicates the following criteria for vocabulary selection:

1. Word frequency
2. Structural value
3. Universality in respect to geographic area
4. Subject range
5. Value for purposes of definition
6. Value for word-building
7. Stylistic function of a word

Mackey suggests terms such as *range, availability,* and *cover-*

age. Range he defines as the number of samples or texts in which an item is found. A word that is found everywhere has far greater importance than one limited to a small range of situations, even though its frequency there may be very high. Availability refers to the usefulness of certain words in given situations. Though *blackboard* and *chalk* are not high-frequency words, they are virtually indispensable in the classroom. The covering capacity of an item refers to the number of things that can be said with it. "It is measured by the number of items which it can displace;"[26] for example, the word *bag* can be used in place of others such as *suitcase*, *valise*, *handbag*, and *sack*.

In addition, it is necessary to distinguish between active and passive vocabularies. In reality there are four kinds of vocabulary. Two, listening and reading, can be termed receptive, passive, or comprehension vocabulary. The other two, speaking and writing, are used for communication and can be called expressive or active vocabulary. Studies have shown that there is considerable difference between the two types of vocabulary.[27]

Moreover, spoken and written vocabularies are also quite distinct, a fact which presents basic problems in using the oral-aural as opposed to a reading approach. Most programs which use a prolonged oral-aural approach but retain reading as a goal, an increasingly uncommon practice in EFL teaching, use both vocabularies. In such courses, the burden of learning the elementary vocabulary is doubled, as courses "covering both areas will do less with either than courses which give primary emphasis to one."[28] One way of bringing the two closer together is to have texts embodying styles, subjects, and vocabularies more similar to normal everyday speech, a trend which is discernible in some newer texts.

With notable exceptions, most modern foreign language texts adhere to the following presentation of materials:

1. Basic conversation sentences
2. Structural notes to help the student perceive and produce speech and sentence patterns
3. Pattern practice to help fix the pattern firmly in mind
4. Laboratory materials for oral-aural practice outside of class
5. More sentences which recombine the parts of the basic sentences for practice and listening[29]

One limitation of this approach is that it tends to give the same amount of practice to easy and difficult problems. Further, it concentrates too much on the memorization of specific sentences and not enough on manipulation of sentence patterns in a variety of semantic situations.[30] In short, dialogues do provide a contextual framework for learning a pattern, but the range of their semantic environments is too limited. In addition, there is no provision enabling students to move from the manipulation of existing material to generating original material.

Underlying the idea of context are Fries's first two principles of language learning: "Things are cognized as wholes . . . we have no ideas not logically associated with others. . . . It being admitted that the thought is the unit of thinking, it necessarily follows that the sentence is the unit of expression." Secondly, "we acquire a knowledge of the parts of an object by first considering it as a whole."[31] To a certain extent, fluency is developed by the ability to recall a model utterance embodying the pattern. Politzer further enlarges the idea of context by stating that "sentences and utterances learned without being associated with anything are not likely to occur to you again,"[32] thus implying the need for a context larger than the sentence.

It is only at a higher level of language organization, the syntactic level, that the opposition of understanding versus memorization becomes significant. Politzer suggests the importance of two seemingly contradictory facts: the more material memorized, the better, and memorization alone does not secure fluency. Even in his native language, a student does not memorize all the sentences he is going to produce. What he does is learn to control a system. Certain modern theories of language, such as transformational grammar, immediate constituent (IC) analysis, and tagmemics, attempt to explain this system. These three theories, although implied in earlier works, did not crystallize until after World War II. Transformational grammar is just beginning to find its place in language teaching. Milka Ivič suggests:

> Syntax is a linguistic discipline which did not begin to develop intensively until the twentieth century. The slow progress of syntactic studies was conditioned by a serious weakness in methodology, which was in general elaborated less thoroughly and with much less sophistication than the methodology relating to phonemics and morphology. . . . The first important innovations in syntax did not appear until the thirties of the present century.[33]

The development and refinement of tagmemics, IC's, and transformational grammar, provide three competing but useful theories on how syntactic structures should be analyzed.

These approaches each provide a basis for different kinds of structural drills.

In tagmemic theory the sentence contains a series of structural slots, each with a certain class of fillers. A tagmeme is the correlation of a grammatical function (slot) with a class of mutually substitutable items (fillers) occurring in that slot.[34] This concept provides the theoretical basis for substitution drills, in which the student is faced with an empty structural slot and is given items for filling it. Slots are recognized at the phrase, clause, and sentence level, while fillers are presented at the word and subword level (for example, affixes and verb roots), though phrases and clauses may also serve as fillers. A slot is represented by a capital letter and a filler by a small one. The occurrence relation between slot and filler is represented as either obligatory ($+$) or optional ($\pm$). Below is a sample of tagmemic analysis, with the sentence containing four slots.

The little boy (1) plays (2) in the field (3) every day (4).

1. Modified count noun phrase $= +$Lim:ar $\pm$M:aj $+$H:nc, where Lim stands for limiter (limiting word), in this case an article (ar). M stands for modifier, here an adjective, and H stands for head word, here a count noun.

2. Predicate $= +$P:vi. The predicate slot is filled by an intransitive verb.

3. Consists of a relater slot manifested by the preposition *in* and an axis slot manifested by a modified count noun. Thus, the phrase is called a location relater-axis phrase (Lra phrase),[35] and is symbolized: $+$R:prep $+$A:mNc, with mNc as a modified count noun.

4. Time $= \pm T:mNc$

Noticing the tagmeme *every day* recalls Palmer's concept of the word in which *yesterday* would be considered a monolog, *every day* a polylog. As fillers, *yesterday* (adverb) and *every day* (a modified count noun) perform the same function in the sentence.

Tagmemic theory underlies the majority of pattern practice exercises that have become the most important single technique in language teaching.[36] The simplest examples of substitution exercises are those in which the filler retains the same structure:

1. | They |
   | I |
   | You |
   | We |
   saw him in the park.

2. We saw | the man |
   | the boys |
   | the dog |
   | the bush |
   in the park.

3. We saw John | near the store. |
   | in the park. |
   | in the library. |
   | at the game. |

The idea of single slots which contain several different constructions carries us over into the area of immediate constituents.

In IC analysis, every structure, or sentence, is divided into immediate constituents, usually two in number. These in turn can be divided until the ultimate constituents, the individual morphemes themselves, have been reached.[37] To show that individual words are insufficient as units for establishing meaning, Charles Hockett cites *a man are*, which by itself is meaningless but which appears in the normal English sentence "The sons and daughters of a man are his children."[38]

The concept of IC's, first suggested by Bloomfield in *Language*, was systematized in the 1940's. IC analysis emphasizes that language does not consist of words strung along in a row but of a complicated nesting of hierarchical structures. IC theory underlies various expansion drills, with the student given a simple structure and then gradually other material which he adds to build more complex structures. Underlying such a drill is the theory that longer sentences are structured the same way as a relatively small number of short sentences or basic sentence types. The way in which longer utterances are built up from the basic sentence types is termed expansion. The patterns common to a large number of sentences of a language are favorite sentence types.[39] The following exercises illustrate the operation of the expansion drill:

1. TCHR: I have to see the man.
   STUD: I have to see the man.
   TCHR: before he leaves
   STUD: I have to see the man before he leaves.
   TCHR: in room 903
   STUD: I have to see the man in 903 before he leaves.
   TCHR: because I have a message for him.
   STUD: I have to see the man in 903 before he leaves because I have a message for him.
2. TCHR: I spoke to him.

STUD: I spoke to him.
TCHR: hardly
STUD: I hardly spoke to him.
3. Also contraction drills:
TCHR: Leave *the other books* on *the desk*.
STUD: Leave the other books on the desk.
TCHR: there
STUD: Leave the other books there.
TCHR: them
STUD: Leave them there.

Used together, IC and tagmemic theory provide a great variety of substitution and expansion drills that help in establishing mastery over specific patterns.

Transformational grammar shares with the teacher a concern for the sequence of presentation.[40] Like tagmemics and IC's, transformational grammar is not basically new, but its systematic arrangement has provided new insights into language.[41] By subsuming both morphology and syntax under a single theory, it eliminates one level of linguistic analysis. Transformational drills include changes from present to past, statement to question, active to passive, and so on. In the transformational approach, the grammarian "tries to discover the small number of core sentences in the language which he can use as raw material to build all the other sentences of the language."[42] In this way, "it is possible to present a great part of the structure of the target language as a series of processes by which a starting sentence is transformed."[43] Attempting to deal with the problem how to produce utterances in a foreign language, Politzer suggests a right and a wrong method. The wrong one involves taking a sentence in the native language, finding individual lexical equivalents in the foreign language, and stringing them together. The right method involves finding a base sentence in the foreign language and converting it into what you want to say.[44] This base sentence has the same syntactic patterns as the final utterance. Thus, with a few changes in lexicon and grammar, in this case the tense of the verb, the base sentence "I was glad that you told him" becomes "I am sorry that you asked him." Basically the model has the same syntactic structure as the final utterance. As language learning continues, the student acquires more and more models so that the number of changes is gradually reduced. In addition, the process is speeded up until it becomes subconscious and automatic as the student approaches fluency.

By revealing differences in structures that seem alike superficially, transformational grammar holds great promise for determining the sequence of patterns. Leonard Newmark suggests that an elementary EFL course include only kernel sentences and that only intermediate and advanced courses contain sentences with the more complex transformations. First the student learns a finite set of elementary constructions and is then taught ways of modifying and joining them into an infinite set of combinations.[45] Newmark further suggests that phonology, according to transformational theory, comes late in constructing the grammar of a language. For this reason, attention to pronunciation could be left until later in the language teaching program—a policy in sharp contrast to the current practice of teaching pronunciation early in the course. "We can often understand a foreign speaker even when he lacks most of the phonological habits of English. . . . It is more important to be able to speak a language and to say a lot of things in it than have marvelous pronunciation but not to know what to say."[46] However, when work on pronunciation is postponed, the student naturally develops a certain accent which ultimately requires far more time to correct than when good habits are established at the beginning.

According to Albert Valdman, the "linguistic method" of language teaching has been most successful at the levels of phonology and morphophonemics, since these two areas can be analyzed "in terms of finite sets of lists readily discoverable by the analyst."[47] The syntactic level is the weakest area of the structural approach, which continues to provide a closed system; the student learns a finite set of basic sentences, which he can vary by substituting lexical items in the slots of the patterns he has learned. However, recent experiments suggest that people do not learn a first language by mimicry and memorization but by constructing from their linguistic environment "a model which can be projected beyond what has been heard in the past to form and recognize new combinations."[48] In further limiting the role of structural linguistics, Sol Saporta states that the learning theory underlying the linguistic concept of language learning is one of stimulus-response formation, in which frequency and reinforcement associated with examples are supposed to ensure the unconscious control of a set of grammatical rules.[49] He questions the validity of this assumption about stimulus-response formation, particularly in the area of meaning; to derive meaning from observing the situation in which it occurs is "quixotic." For an alternative, he turns to the traditional grammarian's approach of attempting to match the two utterances in the native and target languages, while rejecting the application of "relevant abstract formulations"[50] or what we think of as traditional grammar.

A student who makes the most progress in language learning by using rote memory will find the technique hard to abandon and will be prevented from learning the language. From this argument emerges the conflict between transformational analysis and structural linguistics in the teaching of grammar. The structural linguist believes that the rules necessary for creating structural and lexical variants from a basic sentence, if rules they are, will be unconsciously instilled by practicing the pattern itself. Transformationalists, on the other hand, regard language learning as rule-governed behavior, which requires internalizing the rules.[51] In criticizing the structural approach to EFL teaching, Newmark cites the texts of the English Language Institute, stating that the "increase in pattern drill is an index of the return from 'natural' material to grammatical-illustration material."[52] He objects that both traditional and structural textbooks are organized on the basis of linguistic form, which is isolated from its natural context. Newmark does not explain what he means by context, but we can assume that it refers to a semantic environment, something that imparts a wider sense of meaning to the otherwise isolated linguistic structure. However, there is no reason to assume that transformational grammar is better able to provide such a context than structural linguistics. Moreover, some of the more recent EFL texts, such as Praninskas' *Rapid Review of English Grammar*, which follows the structural approach, tend toward a more contextual presentation of grammatical forms. Appendix 4 contains several illustrative lessons which present specific grammatical patterns in a semantic context without recourse to transformational theory.

One obvious fact that transformational grammarians seem to overlook is that in the United States, EFL classes are composed of students with widely differing language backgrounds. Thus, it is impossible to draw on any aspects of translation. Moreover, any lengthy explanation in English is far less likely to be understood than current methods such as acting out meaning, using realia, and presenting sentences in contextual paragraphs. With classes that are linguistically homogeneous, such as may be found overseas, the native language can be used to advantage in explaining grammatical points. In order to determine the value of a grammatical pointer as a strengthening device in review, Marty performed the following experiment in his French class. Students were taught the pattern verb + infinitive. Then the class was divided into two groups for review. In group A review sentences were included in class and on tape but were not underlined. After six weeks tests showed that they did poorly with the structure. With group B the structure was pointed out, and tests showed that the results were excellent for most students.[53]

A final item of considerable importance deals with the problem of manipulation versus communication. The aim of language is communication, urges Prator:

> Until it is used for communicating ideas, it is not language but only parroting; yet many of the textbooks written by some of America's most reputable linguists make little or no provision for communication. There are manipulative exercises galore, but the student is never allowed to have an idea he wishes to convey, to find within himself the necessary words

and the grammatical devices, and to express his thought. . . . The most significant current trend . . . in methods of teaching English as a second language may well prove to be the attempt to assign to communication its proper role in the classroom.[54]

The methodological change from the elementary to the advanced class is the movement from completely controlled responses to increased freedom of expression. Completely controlled responses in beginning classes reduce the chance of errors. Eventually controls must be removed or minimized so that ideas can be formed and presented freely by the student. The entire process is one of gradual transition, whose speed must be controlled by the teacher. Prator suggests a manipulation-communication scale indicating the place of exercises from elementary to advanced skills.[55] Such a scale would have four levels separating the various kinds of exercises:

1. Completely manipulative
2. Predominantly manipulative
3. Predominantly communicative
4. Completely communicative

Levels three and four would correct the greatest deficiency of memorized dialogue material: the lack of provision for eliciting the students' own thoughts and sentences. Dialogues are almost pure manipulation, "since the opportunity for the speakers to supply all or part of the language is practically nil."[56] One particular value of such a scale is that the teacher often uses several different exercises in presenting a grammatical pattern. What often happens is that the exercises vary while the level may not; all of the exercises may remain completely or predominantly manipulative. Once criteria were established for what kind of exercise belonged at each level, it would be easier to design exercises that covered the desired levels. Below is an elaboration of the manipulation-communication categories, with a few illustrative examples of the types of exercises they would contain.

1. *Completely manipulative.* This would include all exercises in which the responses (grammatical and semantic) were completely controlled, for example, most pattern practices with repetition, substitution, and conversion.

Reading passage. The teacher reads a passage sentence by sentence and asks the students wh– and yes/no questions about the material. (See Appendix 4.) The answers are completely controlled and already embedded in the material. This kind of exercise provides the opportunity to move from one level to the next. For example, the teacher uses a story that contains a man driving a car. The aim of the lesson is to teach the subordinate adverb *when*. During or at the end of the story, the teacher asks students, "Do you drive a car?" And if the answer is yes, "How old were you when you learned to drive?" And then a question for another student: "When did Mr. Kajiwara learn to drive?" Mr. Kajiwara's response, "I learned to drive when I was nineteen," is predominantly manipulative but not completely so, for he has had to supply material from his own background, material not given in the lesson. This need to draw from his own experience provides the student a strong bond between the outside world, including the foreign language, and his own interior universe.

2. *Predominantly manipulative.* At this level the grammar

pattern is strictly controlled, but a determined, highly limited amount of semantic material is supplied by the student. For example, a pattern practice substitution exercise from level one can be made predominantly manipulative by allowing the student to provide the missing word. In the sentence "My brother is a doctor," the students supply their own substitutes for *doctor*.

A situation is presented in which there is only one possible answer, although the answer has not been mentioned in class. For example, "Who was the last president of your country?"

3. *Predominantly communicative.* At this level, structures are still controlled but the students now supply most or all of the lexical material, based on their own background or points of view. For example, the teacher presents a selection in the past tense in the same manner as in point one. Then he asks: "What should he have done about the note?" "What would you have done?" "Why?"

a. Using the particular pattern being practiced, the teacher asks about personal preferences or personal activities, being careful not to offend. For example: "What age in the history of the world *would* you *have liked* to live in?" (Several times I have received the answer "The Stone Age.") "What *would* you *be doing* now if you were in [Japan]?" "What did they *teach you to do when* you were a child?" (For a sample lesson, see Appendix 4.)

b. The same principle obtains in preparing a conversation:
(1) There are two roles, A and B. Both are typed out. The teacher (or student I) reads A, and student II reads B. Then they reverse roles.
(2) The students memorize their parts. Student I reads,

and student II responds from memory. Then they reverse. (3) One part, A, is typed out. The teacher or a student reads the part, and another student must create a fill-in conversation.

(4) Or for homework the students are given a sheet with just one part. They have to fill in the empty space with dialogue and bring it to class.

4. *Completely communicative.* This is the hardest level to isolate as a discrete unit and perhaps cannot be fully separated from the previous category. At any level there must be certain controls or limitations—grammatical, semantic, or otherwise—if a class is not to become an informal coffeehouse gathering. The most obvious control is a semantic one in which students are obliged to talk about a certain subject. Lado suggests the use of discussion topics, stories, and film strips as means of controlling free expression.[57] Written material or plain pictures can be used to the same end. Students are given one of the stimuli and are asked to write, talk about, or describe the material. Key questions can guide or direct the discussion.

The manipulation-communication scale can also be used for progressive activities in reading and writing. Corresponding to step one is a presentation with answers found in exact words of the text: complete control. Next comes an exercise in which the information is found in the text but the answer must be rephrased by the student. This would be predominantly manipulative. Finally the students must draw from their own experience; the text is merely suggestive. Such an exercise would be predominantly communicative.

At the lowest level, students can begin writing by copying

existing material, first from the printed page and then from dictation. A form of dictation, useful at the intermediate level and above, is what Robert Ilson calls the dicto-comp, in which the teacher reads a paragraph once or twice.[58] The students listen, then try to reproduce the paragraph verbatim, using the same words and structures and trying to come as close as possible to the original. In a program with separate grammar and vocabulary classes, the paragraph would ideally contain examples of the pattern being practiced in the grammar section. One advantage of presenting written material orally is that students are supplied with the intonation features that are omitted on the printed page. Another approach is assigning two or three pages to be read as homework. The next day the teacher chooses a paragraph of ten or fifteen lines for dictation. In this way the dictation will not contain things the students have not met before. Still another way of dealing with written material orally is to assign to each student a specific paragraph on which he must form five questions. Then in class he may ask other students the questions.

EFL has been guided by certain linguistic theories in the teaching of reading and writing, particularly tagmemic theory. "The prerequisite for rapid reading," states Politzer, "is the quick or instant recognition of the visual symbols expressing structural relationships in the medium of space."[59] In order to develop this ability for recognizing relationships, the teacher can use certain pattern practice exercises: first, using patterns and then partially or completely removing the elements not necessary to convey structural meaning; then gradually introducing the structural frames and having the students supply content words of their own choice.[60]

Writing can be controlled by providing certain key words

that force the student to use a particular form. Time concepts are suitable for this kind of exercise. The student is given a passage to read for homework, for example, on the invention of the electric light. Then the teacher puts the following sentence-opening structures on the board, and the students are asked to write three sentences in each of the corresponding tenses:

1. Before the electric light was invented . . . (simple past)
2. Since then . . . (present perfect)
3. Now . . . (simple present)
4. In the future . . . (simple future)
5. By the year 2000 . . . (future perfect)

Applying the idea of expanding a sentence pattern, the teacher can present a complete piece composed only of simple sentences with no modifiers. The students are then given additional information and have to combine it with the already existing sentences.

Learning a language is more than knowing its forms. It involves a greater understanding of a society's cultural values. A course should contain items that enable foreign students to understand and cope better with the target culture. EFL in this country should include material dealing with American values, customs, and mores. Moreover, although a foreign student can be excused from certain minor breaches of formalities, there are certain rules in every society that cannot be transgressed.

Every society has certain areas of behavior where one has to conform, where the penalties for nonconformity are very severe. Such behavior, moreover, cannot usually be discussed freely in the society. Other areas of behavior, in contrast, are regarded as simply instrumental matters and can be discussed in some if not all social situations. We should teach these distinctions if we are educating for cross-cultural communications.[61]

In addition to the semantic material, there is need for a controlled presentation of structures in the reading material. "Most writers of dialogues and narratives for foreign students have for some time recognized the importance of vocabulary controls, but there has been less recognition of the necessity for controlling sentence patterns. Many books labelled 'Elementary' contain readings in which scant attention has been paid to syntax."[62] Structural simplification should be based on an accumulated inventory of patterns taught up to the time of the reading. The problem is that few, if any, programs have an adequately arranged sequence of patterns from one level to the next. One factor preventing this is the lack of a definitive corpus of English sentence patterns arranged according to some meaningful sequence of presentation.

The language laboratory is chiefly a post–World War II phenomenon, though the use of mechanical recording devices for language teaching goes back to the nineteenth century. Shortly after its invention in 1857, the phonograph was pressed into service as an aid for language teaching. But because of the extremely poor quality of reproduction, these efforts were unsuccessful.[63] In 1908, Abbé Rousselot, a French phonetician, suggested that the phonograph be used for intonation, since its ability to reproduce articulatory differences was still very poor. Jespersen also approved of using the phonograph and pointed out its advantages: it is patient and repeats the same sentences many times without getting tired or changing its intonation, and it enables the students to hear different accents.[64]

In the United States several linguists became interested in the use of machines. Charles C. Clark, a professor of foreign languages at Yale from 1906 to 1918, used phonograph cylinders in teaching pronunciation. In the 1920's several foreign language departments in American universities used phonographs, dictaphones, and similar devices. In 1930, at Ohio State University, Ralph Waltz installed a laboratory that provided the model for all future development. It contained equipment for individual recording, in which students replied to questions and also repeated material after a model. The laboratory was open eleven hours a day and was attended by thirty-five different professors who supervised eight hundred students during the course of the day. It contained essentially the same elements as modern language laboratory programs.[65] Unfortunately, these developments coincided with a period that saw the retreat of the oral approach in the United States and the advance of an emphasis on reading.

Until World War II, work in language laboratories focused mostly on phonetics. Although structuralism appeared early in the century, it did not influence the purpose of the language laboratory until the war. The war period witnessed great progress in electronic technology and in the use of laboratories to teach structure. The postwar period has seen an amazing growth in language laboratories. Between 1945 and 1965 over eight thousand laboratories were installed in the United States, including those in universities, secondary schools, and private organizations.[66] However, many laboratories are not utilized to anywhere near their capacity.

The effective use of a language laboratory depends on five factors:

1. The teacher must have skill and training in the use of equipment.
2. The teaching material must be closely correlated with the classroom materials.
3. Practice sessions must be frequent and long enough to enable students to develop listening and speaking skills.
4. The testing and grading program must give due weight to achievement in listening and speaking.
5. The equipment must be good enough to operate steadily and render reproduction of high quality.[67]

Experiments demonstrate the efficacy of the laboratory in every area of language learning. In order to use the laboratory correctly, the student must understand its separate functions. These functions may be seen to operate in four phases:

1. The listening, recognizing, and understanding phase
2. Pronunciation and the intonation of speech
3. The structural phase: making automatic the grammatical patterns, their arrangement, and their meaning
4. The application or assimilation phase, which has as its ultimate purpose the development of free and fluent oral use of the language[68]

Phase 1. The purpose of phase one is to give students audial drill in the sound system of the language. This includes listening, comprehending, and interpreting the spoken word. It includes exercises in differentiating individual sounds, stress and intonation patterns, and tones and rhythms in the flow of speech. At this level the learning process involves listening to a model, trying to imitate it, and attempting to memorize as much as possible.

Phase 2. The purpose of phase two is to develop the student's ability to express himself in simple everyday conversation. Phase 1 involves learning to distinguish, which is more of a passive-receptive skill, while phase 2 emphasizes the active-productive aspect of pronunciation.

Phase 3. This involves establishing utterances as automatic responses. It also includes training students to manipulate the more frequent syntactic patterns.

Phase 4. Work is devoted to assimilation, application, or synthesis. It involves strengthening the habits already developed during the preceding phases.

These four areas are merely broad principles for the language laboratory program. There are several excellent volumes on methods and materials for the language laboratory.[69] Trends in language laboratory teaching tend to reflect classroom methodology and should benefit considerably from the systematization of syntactic forms in IC, tagmemic, and transformational theory, all of which provide a scientific basis for the treatment of grammatical patterns. In fact, some of the better laboratory material is in advance of classroom procedure because of need in the laboratory for more rigorous control of the elements of stimulus, response, and correction.

The four main skills in language learning are listening, speaking, reading, and writing. All four of these skills can be practiced and developed in the language laboratory. Aside from passive listening, two or more skills are inevitably joined together; listening-speaking, listening-writing, listening-reading-writing. The most important general rule is that lexically and structurally the laboratory material be closely correlated with the work in class. Grammar patterns practiced in the laboratory should be the same as those studied in the classroom. As preparation, brief samples of the drills from the next laboratory period should be given in class. One of the main weaknesses of laboratory material is the poor correlation it often has with classroom work.

The main advantages of the laboratory are (1) it saves time, (2) it allows certain exercises that are far less efficacious if carried on in a classroom, and (3) it has features that combine points one and two. For example, the dicto-comp can be given in the laboratory. Pattern practice exercises are better done in the laboratory, where the student hears his individual response and is not drowned in a sea of voices. Throughout the range of laboratory activities, especially stimulus-response-correction exercises, programmed learning theory becomes particularly relevant because of its insistence on provision for the student to check and correct his responses.

Traditionally, a major concern in the language laboratory has been pronunciation. However, unless the teacher or a trained assistant monitors the student constantly, there is no assurance of pronunciation progress, since the student himself is generally unable to determine the cause of differences between his pronunciation and that on the tape, in such areas as vowel sounds, consonants, linking, rhythm, and stress. Thus, he cannot be sure of correcting himself. One way to provide a check is by forcing the student to make phonemic distinctions. This can be done in several ways. For example, the master tape says a word or a sentence, and the student has a sheet listing words or sentences and must check off the correct one. In contrast to work on phonology, there is a wide range of useful approaches for developing listening comprehension. One is listening to recorded pieces of "real" conversation based on the previously learned structure and lexicon, then several different conversations, each of which rearranges the same structural and lexical material.[70] Another device is recording a lecture or talk on a selected subject, perhaps something already discussed in class, and having students outline it; pick out the main ideas, supporting details, and so forth; write a paragraph on the same subject; or answer questions in writing.*

Practice with grammar drills is the most successful aspect of the language laboratory. All the completely manipulative drills can be used in the laboratory, including an extremely wide variety of pattern practice transformational exercises and dialogues as well. Dialogues should be practiced in an inverse-order technique, presenting the last word first if the utterance can be broken into meaningful parts and then working backward. This method preserves the natural intonation pattern of the sentence. A sentence might be divided in the following way:

. . . please.
. . . butter please.
. . . some bread and butter please.
. . . Bring me some bread and butter please.
. . . Would you bring me some bread and butter please?

If possible, pattern drills should be divided into a teaching phase and a testing phase. In the teaching phase, similar patterns—for example, the object pronouns *it*, *her*, and *him*—are taught separately, while in the testing phase they are all

* For further elaboration, see Stack, *op. cit.*, Chapters 7 and 9.

mixed in together, using some new sentences and others drawn from the teaching phase.

In general, there is an extremely wide range of exercises available for use in the language laboratory, and these exercises can be directed to all four of the major areas of language learning. The general types of drills may be included under the following categories:

1. Recorded conversations
2. Pattern practice
3. Listening comprehension
4. Phonemic discrimination
5. Dictation
6. Directed responses
7. Answering information questions

✺ VII ✺

EFL Teaching Overseas

"In terms of the number of pupils and teachers, of timetable hours and geographic extent, the teaching of English as a second language is the biggest educational undertaking in the world today."[1] United States concern with EFL teaching overseas goes back to the Act for Co-operation with Other American Republics in 1938[2] and has developed immensely since World War II. The United States government and universities and private organizations have sponsored a great range of overseas EFL activities, and many foreign governments have made English an integral part of their university and pre-university curriculum. In West Germany, for example, of the 20 to 30 per cent of secondary school students who prepare for university, 80 per cent study English as their first foreign language, while in Japan, seven million children and 600,000 university students, nearly the entire student population, are studying English. Educational statistics for the Soviet Union show that in 1959–60 three-quarters of all students in higher education studied English, with 12,400 college students training to be teachers, translators, or interpreters of English.[3] In France, 60 per cent of secondary school students begin English in their first year, while only 23 per cent study German.[4]

There are three broad reasons why countries may need a foreign or second language:

1. In newly emerging nations, the need to develop cadres of highly trained personnel, particularly in science, technology, and economics, and to meet the constant demands of information flow.

2. In multilingual countries such as India, Nigeria, and others in Asia and Africa, the need for a common language in such fields as education, administration, communications, and business.

3. International contact—in political and cultural affairs, international business, and general intercourse with foreign nations.

Even in these three categories, English assumes varying significance in different nations. For example, in the former East African countries of Kenya, Uganda, and Tanganyika, it is a mark of additional education. It is introduced in late primary school, adopted as the medium of instruction at the secondary level, and used extensively in higher education. Although secondary school enrollment is low,[5] English has been designated as the official national language, making it essential for positions in government. Older leaders, unable to read or speak English, find themselves cut off from participation in national affairs. Because of the linguistic situation, however, no other official language seems feasible. Only three of the nearly two hundred vernaculars in East Africa are spoken by over one million people. Swahili, the only widespread language—with seven million speakers—is the native language of no one and is inadequate for international communication and higher education.

India, with its fifteen major languages and hundreds of dialects, provides a classic example of a country with need for a second language. Because of the bewildering linguistic diversity of the country, English plays the role of a *lingua franca*. Examinations for military commissions and the National Civil Service are given in English.[6] Although Hindi is the national language, it is spoken by less than one-third of the people,[7] and the government has tried to promote a policy of using three languages: English, Hindi, and a regional language (when it differs from Hindi). This three-language policy is gradually being introduced on signs along national and state highways.[8] Actually, English pervades many areas of modern Indian society. Big business firms require employees, except at the lowest levels, to be competent in English. English is used for legal transactions in all but the smallest hamlets and remains the language of science and technology. Even truck drivers and mechanics need enough English to cover the technical aspects of their work.[9]

In the Philippines, on the other hand, English is the only common language and the only one regularly taught beyond the third grade. Thus, with only 38 per cent of the population able to speak it, English begins to pass from a foreign to an upper-class, second language to a mass language.[10]

In some ways, "English today enjoys a position which makes it best suited of the world's major languages to meet the communication requirements of almost all the countries which must establish wider and more effective contact with the rest of the world."[11] Only a few languages are used extensively for international communication. The United Nations recognizes five: English, French, Spanish, Russian, and Mandarin Chinese. Of these, Chinese, including all dialects, has the greatest number of speakers, about 680 million,[12] but its geographic spread is relatively limited and its writing system extremely difficult even for native speakers. Second, with about 260 million native speakers, is English, which accounts for 62 per cent of all scientific writing.[13] Although fifth, seventh, and eleventh respectively in native speakers, Russian, German, and French (and possibly Japanese) are the only other languages with enough scientific writing to meet all the needs of the emerging countries.

The more readily English is made available, the closer the contact between developing nations and the West. At present, even the combined resources of all the English-speaking countries are inadequate to provide the materials, texts, and teachers needed to meet world-wide demands.[14] These demands have stimulated considerable growth in American university programs for training EFL teachers. The programs, which emphasize applied linguistics, attract a fairly high percentage of foreign teachers. In 1963 nineteen universities offered degrees in teaching English as a foreign language, and sixteen others offered courses.[15] This is in addition to degrees offered in linguistics. For the nature and scope of the EFL degree the reader is directed to a 1966 publication of the Center for Applied Linguistics.[16] Ultimately, the solution to world EFL needs lies in providing foreign teachers with a high degree of training.

One method of determining the EFL needs of a country is through a survey conducted by specialists in several fields, to establish the nature, scope, and feasibility of a prospective EFL program. The survey would include such things as

size, cost, local teachers available, and so forth.[17] A broad
range of factors must be taken into account when establishing
an EFL program, including:

1. Degree of illiteracy. High illiteracy suggests a need for
learning the local language before English. Accordingly, English would probably be offered to a specific segment of the
population rather than the general public.

2. Linguistic unity. A country with one national language
offers problems and opportunities different from one with
several regional languages. For example, one national language allows for the use of contrastive analysis and a single
set of materials. The existence of four or five major languages
requires a different approach in designing materials.

3. Position of English. Is it a firmly established second language used in the country, or is it taught only in school? As
a widely used medium, it is best introduced at the lower levels.

4. Institutional rivalries. Are there conflicting programs of
various local and foreign organizations?[18]

A national sociolinguistic profile might also include the following:

5. The pattern of language dominance. In Afghanistan, for
example, Persian and Pashto are spoken by roughly equal
numbers of people. But Persian is learned as a second language
by Pashto speakers, while Pashto as a second language is
highly limited, despite official government support.[19]

Further considerations that tend to arise in overseas programs
are:

6. Classroom facilities. Is there electricity for a language
laboratory? Can one be sure of such things as blackboards

and chalk, English language newspapers and magazines with pictures?

7. Extent of the student's contact with English. Is it ever used on radio or television? Are American and British films widely shown? Are other courses taught in English? Where and to what extent is English used in the country?

8. Teachers who will ultimately carry on the program. What is their level of education, their training in linguistics and language teaching? What is their competence in English? What is the status of teachers in the country?

9. The background and cultural values of the country. This is particularly useful in determining subject matter to be taught. It makes little sense, linguistically or otherwise, to discuss superhighways with students in a pre-industrial, agrarian society. It is a heavy burden, learning new grammatical and cultural concepts at the same time. In choosing subject material, it is often very useful to draw examples from the student's own environment, especially if it is markedly different from American or western European patterns.

10. The students. What is their educational background? What is the role of English in particular, and education in general, in their future opportunities? How many teaching days, or class sessions, can the teacher be reasonably sure of? What is the normal class size?

Programs should also be planned with different services and goals in mind. Without specific goals, the EFL program may continue as a potpourri of unrelated activities and become a perpetuating self-interest on the part of the contracting agency. Typical of a project with definite aims was the University of Michigan Southeast Asia program, which ran from

August, 1958, to June, 1964. Its purpose was to improve the teaching of English through the following activities: a contrastive analysis of English and the native languages; preparation of teaching materials based on the contrastive analysis; in-service and pre-service training in Southeast Asia; selection of participants for advanced training at the University of Michigan; and consultant services by the University of Michigan staff.[20]

One of the greatest problems in overseas EFL programs is lack of continuity. Sometimes project funds are cut off too soon for a program to take effect. Often change of staff within the same project results in scrapping one development project and instituting another. One way to solve this problem is to commit administrative personnel for longer periods of from three to eight years. Unfortunately, project directors are often hired for a specific program and are not guaranteed security on their return to the United States. If the project is directed by an American university, administrators can be drawn from the regular teaching staff. The aspect of administrative continuity poses major problems with EFL staffs working for the United States government, as few of the various government positions carry career opportunities with long-range retirement benefits.[21]

Another problem facing overseas EFL programs is suspicion by many natives, who regard the projects, especially those associated with the United States government, as a form of propaganda. For this reason, different types of contract agencies may prove suitable for different situations. For example, for teaching small groups such as police, airport personnel, or cabinet officials, a private commercial enterprise seems most appropriate. In co-operating with foreign education systems, the American university offers in-depth experience with comparable programs. On the other hand, for dealing with the general public, United States government agencies can provide the broadest range of EFL services.[22]

Many American organizations, both public and private, are involved in EFL teaching overseas. Private organizations include English Language Services, Electronic Teaching Laboratories, and big corporations such as Caltex and the Arabian-American Oil Company. Nonprofit groups involved in EFL overseas include the Ford and Asia foundations, Asia Society, the International School Foundation, the Lauback Literacy Fund, the African-American Institute, and the Rockefeller Foundation.[23] American government participation is seen most clearly in five areas: the State Department, which has cultural exchange programs, including linguistics and teaching EFL for foreign students and teachers; the United States Information Service, which has EFL teaching as a part of its program to develop understanding of American culture; the Agency for International Development, which has EFL teaching as part of its technical assistance programs; the Military Assistance Advisory Group, which provides English instruction to foreign military personnel; and the Peace Corps.[24]

In 1960 the USIS conducted EFL courses in eighty-three countries and, along with the Binational Centers, taught English to over 190,000 students.[25] In fiscal 1961 the number of students was 221,162. The USIS employed 3,245 American and foreign teachers and conducted 141 workshops organized for 9,000 teachers of English.[26] By 1965 the number of students had risen to about 250,000.[27]

In conjunction with the Military Assistance Advisory Group, the Defense Language Institute (Department of Defense) teaches English to foreign military personnel in the United States and overseas. When a foreign government receives military supplies, the United States government also provides training for utilization and maintenance. In order to meet the needs of the training program, which is in English, the Defense Language Institute (DLI) provides English instruction for the trainees, who usually number about 100,000 a year. The DLI offers intensive four- to six-month courses in forty-eight countries.[28]

But the program involving the most Americans teaching EFL overseas is the Peace Corps. In one way or another, almost all of the 8,000 Peace Corpsmen are teaching EFL on a part- or full-time basis, either in schools or incidentally in their everyday activities.[29] During their three-month training program, most volunteers receive about one hundred hours instruction in EFL methodology, including practice teaching. Of the total group, 849 corpsmen are engaged specifically in teaching EFL.[30]

A great deal of EFL teaching is done overseas by countries other than the United States, particularly Great Britain, which from its long association with India and Africa has produced a considerable amount in the area of methods and materials. Discussion of these activities would make a study in itself, but it is interesting that until quite recently the British have tended to neglect applied linguistics in favor of more traditional approaches to language teaching. Commonwealth nations tend to favor the following:

1. The use of English as a medium for teaching other subjects and the teaching of English for its future use as a medium in education.

2. The resulting close integration between the aims of English teaching and the general education aims.

3. Transfer of content and methodology, especially at the secondary level, derived from teaching English or the classics in Britain.

4. Transfer of British examinations and examination-directed syllabuses overseas, again especially at the secondary level.

5. Heavy emphasis on controlled reading, often a study of English literature, and on composition writing.[31]

As we have seen, EFL programs overseas involve certain practical considerations quite different from programs in the United States. Some of these considerations are extra-linguistic, while others bear directly on methodology and materials involved in the language class. But the greatest difference between EFL operations in America and overseas lies in the students' language background; in a foreign country, students usually have the same native language, while in the United States, classes contain students with a wide variety of native languages. When there is only one native language to deal with, contrastive analysis can be used in structuring materials. Essentially, contrastive analysis involves the following operations: analysis of the student's native language (phonology, syntax, and so on); analysis of comparable elements in English, the target language; comparison of these elements in the two languages to determine problems and interference caused by the native language in learning the target language.* Until recently, contrastive analysis has been

* For contrastive studies of particular languages, see John H. Hammer and Frank A. Rice, *A Bibliography of Contrastive Linguistics.*

used chiefly at the phonological level.[32] However, this technique can be extended to higher levels of language structure. A problem at the grammatical level is whether differences and similarities between two systems should be stated in terms of tagmemes, grammatical categories, sentence types, or kernel sentences. "The cause of specific interference phenomena can, in most cases be determined by linguistic methods: If the phonic or grammatical systems of two languages are compared and their differences delineated, one ordinarily has a list of the potential forms of interference in the given contact situation."[33]

The general phonological problem in foreign language learning is that "the speaker of one language, listening to another, does not actually hear the foreign language sound units. . . . He hears his own,"[34] especially with similar sounds that differ only in small phonetic details. Moreover, "when a phoneme in the foreign language does not exist in the native language the student will tend to substitute the native phoneme that seems nearest within the whole structure of his native language."[35] Furthermore, in a contrastive analysis of two languages, distribution is as important as the catalog of phonemes. For example, English does not conjoin the consonant sequence *mb* in the same syllable or in word-initial position, whereas Swahili does contain *mb* word-initially.[36] Thus, the *mb* in word-initial position represents a potential source of difficulty for a speaker of English who is learning Swahili.

Overseas, English is often needed chiefly as a tool for reading technical material, textbooks, and other printed matter. In the United States this is rarely the goal of an EFL course. A widely accepted dictum is that development of oral mastery is the best approach, even for those learning to read. How does this dictum affect the organization of a course whose main aim is reading mastery? Certain elements of pronunciation relate directly to reading development. For the learner the written language becomes a kind of phonetic system, and without some knowledge of that system the reader is hindered in his comprehension. But in a situation where reading is the goal, "no complete and thorough-going pronunciation course will be found to be necessary, and only those sounds which a collection of 'errors' or departures from the norm, and a contrastive analysis show to be likely to cause a potential breakdown of communication, will be included in the course."[37] Carroll uses the terms *convergent* and *divergent* to describe the ways two languages treat similar segments. A convergent phenomenon is one in which two or more symbols in the native language are represented by a smaller number of symbols in the target language, while a divergent phenomenon is one in which the target language contains a greater number of symbols and semantic distinctions than the native language.[38] Divergent items are more important for the student as a speaker, convergent items more critical for him as a listener. Divergent differences are also harder to learn, as they require a selective response. Both kinds of differences exist in morphology and syntax, as well as in lexicon.

A surprisingly neglected area is contrastive meaning analysis. Words in the native and target language may correspond in one context and be totally inappropriate in others. For example:

> I can do this *too*.
> I can do this *also*.

Too can also be used in the sentence "This is much *too* hard," whereas "This is much *also* hard" is not a grammatical English sentence.[39] Similarly:

> He *got out* of the country.
> He *left* the country.

Using the first verb in a different context, we have "What did you *get out* of the book?" while "What did you *leave* of the book?" makes no sense to us. Contrastive meaning analysis thus requires examples of words in as many contexts as possible. Relative meanings can be further demonstrated by overlapping circles. Rather than one meaning, a word has a range of meanings that fall within circle A, while a semantically similar word in another language has a range that falls within circle B. Two terms may have a certain amount of overlap, or congruent meanings (the shaded area), and certain areas of no relation. Distinguishing overlap and difference can help greatly in the teaching of vocabulary.

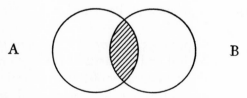

Contrastive meaning analysis further deals with the semantic conditioning of grammatical forms. For example, consider the verb *to have* in English and Hindi. Hindi depends on certain criteria that are grammatically and semantically non-significant in English:

1. "I have a book" is, in Hindi, *"Meeree pas eek kitaab*

*hai,"** literally, "With me there is a book." *Meeree pas* is used
with tangible objects personally owned or possessed.

2. "I have a daughter." In Hindi: *"Meerii eek laRkii hai,"*
literally, "My daughter there is." *Meerii* is used for the possession of people: relatives, parents, parts of the body.

3. "I have a clothing store." In Hindi: *"Meeree pas kapRee
ki dukaan hai"* or *"Meerii kapRee ki dukaan hai."* Both forms
can be used with larger objects such as cars, houses, stores, and
so forth.

4. "I have a cold." In Hindi: *"Mujh ko buxaar hai,"* literally, "To me there is a cold." *Mujh ko* is used for abstract
objects that are possessed (ideas, feelings, maladies) rather
than concrete objects.[40]

The distinction between lexical and grammatical elements is
not always a sharp one, and lexical items in one language
become grammatical in another. Take, for example, the English sentence "It is my book." In English there are four discrete lexical items, whereas in Persian there is only one word,
/kitabemanast/, in which *kitab = book*; *man = me* (or *I*);
–e– = a possessive particle; and *ast = he, she,* or *it is.* In this
case the morphological and syntactic elements should be separated and drilled for the speaker of Persian learning English.

A final point on contrasting the grammatical structures of
two languages: the grammatical system of English makes
certain distinctions but not others. For example, the verbal system contains *I write* and *I am writing.* French employs no
such distinction. In contrasting structures, one can compare
the way the two languages arrange similar items, such as

---

* I have followed the modified phonetic transcription used in John
Gumperz and June Rumery, *Conversational Hindu-Urdu.*

plurals, possessives, structures of modification, question words, concord, word order as a grammatical device, and the ways different structures are combined into single units.* Lado recommends a general approach to preparing a contrastive structure analysis:

1. Locate the best structural descriptions of the languages involved.
2. Summarize in a compact outline all of the structures.
3. Make an actual comparison, pattern by pattern.

Items two and three, of course, represent a major investment in time and energy and would be extremely ambitious in anything less than a really large-scale language teaching project. In connection with items one and two, transformational analysis offers a basis for comparing the kernel sentences in two languages.

* A suggested list of items for comparison is contained in Lado, *Linguistics Across Cultures*, 51–74. The reader is also referred to some of the excellent exploratory studies in the University of Chicago Contrastive Structure Series.

☙ VIII ☙

Conclusion

IT IS A LONG distance from Quintilian's Rome to twentieth-century America, but in language teaching, as in other areas of man's endeavors, history preserves. "Many techniques which are used today have been tried in the past and several have been 'rediscovered' more than once."[1] From the standpoint of synchronic language analysis,* little of a linguistic nature was done between Quintilian's time and the nineteenth century. But an increasingly rigorous scientific spirit, coupled with more and more information on non-Indo-European languages, eventually brought about a revolution in the study of language and language units. The main value of this understanding to language teaching was an insistence that grammar be derived from careful observation of the structure of a language itself, not from some a priori notions of Latin grammatical forms. Such a conclusion was reached as early as the eighteenth century by Joseph Priestly, but not until the twentieth century did its full significance become apparent

* Synchronic linguistics studies a language at only one stage of development and is not concerned with historical changes in the language (diachronic linguistics).

as a result of work by linguists such as Boas and Bloomfield. Once freed from the shackles of a universal grammar, language analysis probed farther and farther into the structure of language, its components, and the ways it operates. From Baudouin de Courtenay came the notion of the phoneme, which provided the chief tool of linguistic investigation until the 1930's. From studies in structural linguistics emerged a greater understanding of grammatical form in language, an understanding further enlarged by such concepts as tagmemics and immediate constituent analysis. At the sentence level, transformational grammar has offered fresh insight into the nature of the complete utterance.

All of these concepts—structural linguistics and the phoneme, IC analysis, tagmemics, and transformational grammar —have added considerably not only to our understanding of language but to the methodology of teaching it. Nowhere have these theories been applied more directly than in English as a foreign language. Parker suggests that "recent experiences in teaching English as a foreign language give promise of improved techniques for the teaching of foreign languages to Americans."[2]

Language teaching using an oral-aural method in contextual (that is, semantically connected) utterances of greater than sentence length goes back to Greek-Latin texts of the third century B.C. The two approaches, oral-aural work and connected utterances, were often used in later centuries by such illustrious masters as Erasmus and Comenius. But by the eighteenth century, as Latin ceased to be taught as a living language, the grammar-translation method came to replace the oral-aural approach to language teaching. This heritage, carried over from the Old World, dominated foreign-language teaching in the United States during the nineteenth and early part of the twentieth century. However, by virtue of its being a native language in the United States, English was subject to considerations somewhat different from those of foreign languages taught in schools and colleges. Foreigners or immigrants studying English in American schools had an eminently practical purpose: to communicate with native speakers of the language in everyday situations. This was no intellectual exercise with literary embellishments. Few of these people had time for such things. They needed a direct, immediate command of the spoken language. Thus, a different methodology was necessitated, one better suited to these aims. The best way of learning to speak is by speaking. This seemed the most logical assumption, and since the grammar-translation method offered little guidance, EFL teachers turned to François Gouin, whose oral method of foreign language teaching had become quite popular.

During the first three decades of the twentieth century, EFL teaching was stimulated by the great number of non-English-speaking immigrants. Most texts of the time were built around a topical subject (subject oriented) rather than a grammatical pattern (pattern oriented) and had inadequate provisions for drill on specific patterns. From 1920 on, the increasing number of foreign students at colleges and universities also necessitated the inclusion of EFL courses at the college level. The number of foreign college students reached 10,000 by 1929 but dropped to just under 5,000 as a result of the depression. The number once again reached 10,000 in 1945 and has been climbing steadily ever since as more and more of the newly emerging countries send students abroad to learn the technical skills necessary for building a nation.

Conclusion

This burgeoning foreign-student population, the ASTP experience in language teaching, and developments in the field of linguistics combined to produce new directions in EFL teaching. Programs were organized with separate but co-ordinated grammar, vocabulary, and pronunciation classes at the same level. In an approach of this sort, the topic, for example, might be "The World of the Future." The grammar class would be devoted to the future tense, and the vocabulary class would teach words from the grammar lesson, such as computer, atomic power, speed, airplanes, communication, shortage, while the pronunciation class would drill on the future tense in affirmative statement, negative, and question forms, also utilizing the lexical items from the vocabulary lesson. Programs have increased in the number of levels and number of hours per week, and testing techniques for determining class level have become more rigorous. However, there is still much to be desired in areas such as placement testing.

A persistent problem is determining the content of course levels. Assuming a program has three levels, arbitrarily beginning, intermediate, and advanced, how can they be arranged so that there is no overlap between them? The best way to do this is by establishing a complete inventory of the patterns, or structures, and apportioning them according to the time available at each level. This has yet to be done. One thing that prevents such an undertaking is the lack of a definitive analysis of the English language. Admittedly, such a project would require an enormous amount of work but, once accomplished, could provide a common point of reference for the otherwise hopelessly diverse EFL texts now being published. The tenets of foreign-language teaching may never become as sharply defined as the periodic table in chemistry, but certain broad areas of agreement have emerged, and these areas must be refined further in order to produce as scientific an approach as possible in a field which has tended to be an art.

Appendix 1. Development of EFL Courses, 1880-1940

SINCE PROGRAMS differed from city to city and state to state, it is hard to generalize. Evening school terms varied widely, from Traverse City, Michigan, with 20 sessions, one a week, to Los Angeles and Oakland, with 187 sessions, five a week. Larger cities tended to have longer sessions. Certain similarities were apparent within states. For example, California varied between 140 and 187 sessions, evening school almost coexistent with the day school; Connecticut schools had 75 sessions a year, and New Jersey, 64.[1] In a Bureau of Education national survey, 1914–16, the following distribution appeared among 374 cities responding to a questionnaire:[2]

1 night per week	5
2 nights per week	54
3 nights per week	175
4 nights per week	102
5 nights per week	38

Individual states became increasingly concerned with the problem of teaching English as a foreign language. A report of the New York State Education Department from 1911 outlines the following: "The policy of the State should be to require all cities having a certain number of foreign adults who have declared their intention to become citizens to maintain night schools wherein such persons may be taught the English language and American History. Special apportionment of State funds in support of these schools should be authorized."[3] However, not until 1915 did New York begin to take a strong interest in the problem. At that time it conducted a brief survey of needs and facilities, which resulted in the publication of several bulletins for use by local school authorities. The bulletin devoted to EFL methods used the Gouin approach,[4] as did bulletins of many other states. In 1917 a full-time supervisor was appointed to help co-ordinate evening school efforts. Training courses were set up by the state, and thousands of teachers given special instruction on Americanization and EFL teaching.[5] But the problem was most acute in New York City, the great immigration center of the nation. Although enrollment in New York City evening schools in 1914–15 reached 36,923, with the figure rising steadily,[6] the 1920 census revealed 208,125 foreign-born whites ten years and older unable to speak English.[7] Prevalent practice in city schools was reflected in comments of those intimately connected with the problem:

> The teacher generally begins the evening's work with a conversation. The subject may be on a prepared theme or topic of current interest. Students do oral reading which is corrected by the teacher. In writing, the pupils drill on forms, copy from the board, write from memory, and only lastly, do original work. (Robert B. Brodie, Principal, Manhattan Public Evening School No. 2.)

The main interest of immigrants in evening schools is learning to converse in English. This interest covers: (1) a number of ideas, (2) sufficient vocabulary to express the ideas, and (3) a manner of expression that will enable others to understand. Most adult immigrants between 20 and 50 have their own ideas. Hence, the main purpose is to provide an equivalent vocabulary and ways of expressing those words. Vocabulary is taught from realia: by naming objects in the classroom, etc. Translation into the student's language is not permitted; an attempt is made to establish a direct association or connection between the object and the symbol representing it in English. Then, names of objects, actions, qualities of objects, and idiomatic expressions are gradually introduced. (Isador Springer, Principal, Brooklyn Public Evening School No. 144.)[8]

Our first business is to teach English, the colloquial English that will enable a man to go on in life; to get a job, to keep it, and then to get a better one . . . to overcome that feeling of strangeness. . . . No other phase of instruction should be allowed to interfere with this primary one. (Albert Shields, District Superintendent, New York City Schools.)[9]

Another state active in EFL teaching was Massachusetts, with classes in Boston going back as far as 1885. But, as in most states, the greatest development occurred in the first two decades of the twentieth century. In 1919 the Massachusetts commissioner of education issued bulletins containing plans and suggestions for immigrant education, with teacher-training classes held by the Department of University Extension.[10] Considerable concern for immigrant education and EFL teaching was also shown after World War I, as reflected in the following statement from a Massachusetts Department of Education bulletin:

The term "Americanization" . . . in its widest significance . . . means making good American citizens of both native and foreign-born. . . . In so far . . . as this task has to do with foreigners . . . that achievement will be delayed as long as millions . . . are separated from us by a language barrier. The teaching of our . . . language has accordingly come to be regarded as the first and . . . one of the most important steps in the Americanization process.[11]

The bulletin further acknowledged the need for highly skilled teaching and for teacher training, plus the increasing importance of factory classes. An EFL teacher's handbook issued by the Board of Education was based on the Gouin theme method[12] and refers also to the work of Goldberger. The following chart showing the precipitous growth in EFL classes between 1918 and 1923 also contains figures on other organizations involved in EFL activities:[13]

Year	1918–19	1919–20	1920–21	1921–22*
Immigrants in all classes	3,381	9,030	20,475	22,242
Number of evening school classes		420	750	855
Number of factory classes		131	327	366
Others: neighborhood, club classes		92	248	294

* Total enrollment increased to 27,000 in 1922–23.

In Connecticut, laws governing evening school classes for non-English-speaking adults stipulated that every town with over 100,000 people should establish and maintain evening schools and that there should not be fewer than seventy-five sessions of two hours each per week.[14] A state bulletin on classes for foreigners emphasizes the fact that teaching English to foreigners is a "highly specialized phase of pedagogy" and "it is not always true that the competent day school teacher is qualified to teach English to non-English-speaking adults."[15] The bulletin suggests two criteria for establishing courses: one based on the level of competence—elementary, intermediate, and advanced; the other, if numbers justify it, based on nationality. Unfortunately, the reason for this was not to exploit linguistic homogeneity but to avoid racial prejudice and help newcomers feel at home.[16] The bulletin further restricts classes to twenty-five students, recommending three or four meetings a week—two-hour sessions three times a week or one- to one-and-a-half-hour sessions four times a week.[17] Another bulletin containing a suggested EFL syllabus and course of study follows the Gouin theme method of teaching.[18] Sentences in the theme are contextual; that is, they all refer to a similar subject. However, there is little controlled presentation of verb forms, except that all the tenses are limited to the infinitive or simple form of the verb, such as *he goes, he wants to go, he will go, he can go, he must go.*

Among the earliest states to develop EFL courses for immigrants was Pennsylvania, which authorized public evening elementary schools for adults as far back as 1842.[19] In 1850, Philadelphia conducted eight evening classes in EFL which ran from January to late March, with three sessions a week. Pittsburgh established classes in 1855, Erie in 1869, and Scranton in 1878. At first, ordinary day-school textbooks were used. But in 1902, J. B. Richey, superintendent of schools at McKeesport, introduced special texts adapted for immigrants.[20] In 1907 a law was passed specifically establishing "schools for adults, including foreigners."[21] In 1925 regular state certification of teachers went into effect, and public EFL classes were made part of the state system. World War I hastened the growth of similar courses throughout the state, with the Pennsylvania Department of Public Instruction occasionally issuing bulletins describing courses and related methodology. One such bulletin suggests that teachers be grounded in the direct method, the conversational method, and the Gouin method. It emphasizes that the translation method is never used and that "no printed or written material should be given to them [the students] until the English oral symbols employed have been directly associated with their respective meanings."[22] The size of the problem facing the state may be indicated by the following figures. In 1910 there were 1,436,719 foreign-born whites in Pennsylvania, 19.3 per cent of the total white population.[23] English illiteracy among foreign-born whites was 466,825, constituting 33.6 per cent of the foreign-born population. The same year showed school attendance among foreign-born at 69,257, divided into the following categories: ten years and over, 45,640; fifteen years and over, 10,804; and twenty-one years and over, 2,894. Although many foreigners attended classes, the schools never really reached the great majority of foreigners in any state. In 1914 there were 9,087 foreigners enrolled in evening classes in Philadelphia. Nevertheless, by 1920 there were still 31,742 adults in Philadelphia unable to speak English.[24]

Similar conditions existed in other urban centers. Between 1910 and 1915 the foreign-born population of Detroit increased 300,000. Starting in 1915, public and private organizations, the chamber of commerce, the city government, school departments, and churches, all joined together in a situation where English-speaking citizens were actually outnumbered by those of alien tongues.[25] Appropriations were secured, teachers selected and trained, and workers urged by their employers to join classes. A publicity campaign conducted by the press resulted in a 153 per cent increase in evening school classes over the previous year. A supervisor of immigrant education was appointed to train teachers in methods, select appropriate courses and texts, and co-ordinate the work of various schools and organizations.[26] Yet, by 1915, EFL enrollment was only 11,000, little more than 5 per cent of those who could have profited from instruction.[27]

Outside the eastern and midwestern states, California was also quite active in the field of English for foreigners and was even in advance of other states in some of its methodology. A state bulletin on immigration education gives the following order of presentation in teaching the EFL lesson: listening while the teacher gives a sentence and dramatizes the meaning; speaking, first in class as a group, then individually; reading; and writing.[28] The bulletin points out that the "pupil should never be allowed to see the written word before he hears it and uses it *orally himself.*"[29] These excerpts suggest the general approach of the book:

> The purpose of language, a modern language, and emphatically the purpose of acquiring the English language for practically every student in night school, is not to become familiar with English literature, but to be able to communicate with his fellows.

> We do not learn to speak except by speaking. Years of night school reading and writing will contribute practically nothing to the power of using English orally. We do not learn to speak by

hearing the teacher talk or by spelling or by reading from a book, or by any other method than by talking.[30]

In order to facilitate language learning, sentences should be concerned with a single topic. The author suggests choosing a definite topic for each lesson and cautions that unrelated sentences are confusing to less advanced students. Ideally, a topic should concern itself with an experience common to the students and should involve something they have need to talk about. For example, we all get up in the morning, wash our faces, and walk to the door, but we usually do not talk about these things; whereas we do speak of going to the bank and making a deposit. This realization is a big step beyond the Gouin-Goldberger sentences, which deal with a demonstrable environment but not one that people necessarily talk about. Moreover, the material learned, such as structures and lexicon, should be immediately useful in real situations. In a lesson on the streetcar, it is more helpful to understand "Fares please," "Transfers please," "Let me off at . . ." than to produce phrases like "I stop the car," "I get on," "I walk to the seat."[31] Reading is regarded as supplementary, never as the main work of the evening. The teacher prepares the students for reading by presenting the subject matter and teaching the lexicon and structures beforehand in sentences. "The student should not encounter a new word for the first time in reading, but should already be familiar with it orally."[32] Aside from copying down parts of the evening lesson, writing should be confined to the students' actual writing needs—checks, receipts, and perhaps business letters. Only in advanced classes should more time be devoted to reading and writing.

Following is a typical lesson in another California bulletin on teaching EFL to beginners in rural schools:

Buying Coveralls

Saturday afternoon. I go to the store.

CLERK: Good afternoon.
MR. B: I want a pair of coveralls.
CLERK: What size?
MR. B: I want size 34.
CLERK: Blue or tan?
MR. B: I want blue coveralls.
CLERK: This is a good pair.
MR. B: How much?
CLERK: This pair is $7.50.
MR. B: I want this pair.[33]

Then, under a section called Structure Drills is the pattern "How much is . . . ?" and another section with specific questions: "How much is a pair of overalls?" "a pair of gloves?" "a rake?" For teaching the lesson, the bulletin advises that, if possible, the teacher should bring pictures of the activities, then step by step:

1. The teacher says the sentence and the students listen.
2. The class repeats the sentence two or three times.
3. Several individuals say the sentence.
4. The teacher writes the sentence on the blackboard.
5. The teacher dramatizes the sentence with pictures and other things.
6. The teacher acts one role, a student the other.
7. Students practice different roles.
8. Students read the sentence(s) from a book or from the board.
9. Structure drills: old vocabulary is practiced.[34]

The state also produced some interesting texts. One, for example, for intermediate and advanced students, was on California history from pre-Spanish times to 1934. Various questions following the reading were designed to "give the student the opportunity to use in his answers the vocabulary and structures of the lessons as well as to test comprehension. . . . The important thing is not whether he can define a given word or idiom or 'tell what it means.' The important thing is his ability to *use* it."[35] Each lesson is divided into two parts: a reading selection and a series of extremely useful exercises:

1. Combining pairs of sentences by using participles, infinitives, and other forms. In these exercises, students were given pairs of sentences and were told to combine them by using a specific grammatical form.

2. Completing the following with facts from the lesson:
   a. After many weeks . . .
   b. For two centuries . . .
   c. During the sixteenth century . . .

3. Then completing the above with facts *not* from the lesson.

4. Word study. Answering questions using the underlined words:
   a. Name two countries that have *colonized* Africa.
   b. Name a European country not on the *mainland* of Europe.[36]

5. Using a specific word instead of the general term that is underlined:
   a. India was a land of *rich treasures* (gold, silver, ivory).
   b. India was rich in *precious stones* (diamonds, emeralds, and so forth).

6. The same exercise as above, but the students must replace specific words with more general terms.

7. Students have to fill in blanks with a specific form, for example, the gerund:
   a. The boys wasted much time in . . .
   b. After . . . here ten years, the family moved away.
   c. Upon . . . her freedom from Spain, Mexico took control of California.

Appendix 2. Analysis of Early EFL Texts

APPENDIX 2 examines the methodology and design of the EFL texts most popular from 1900 to 1920.

The earliest volume is William E. Chancellor's *Reading and Language Lessons for Evening Schools*, in which the author explains his method as one of "the word, with the object represented pictorially."[1] In all the lessons, "talking the language precedes writing it,"[2] but no directions are offered for developing an oral approach.

Basically, the volume is divided into two parts: reading for adult beginners and lessons in language. Each of the twenty lessons contains the statement "Study page X," which refers to a particular reading passage, accompanied by a picture. After studying the passage, students are directed to answer the questions, with no indication whether this should be done in oral or written form. Students are then asked to describe the picture. In addition to a reading passage, the day's lesson includes a chapter from *Lessons in Language* dealing with some grammatical feature. Again there is little correlation between the grammar section and the reading passage. Lesson Three, for example, contains six reading passages on various topics. The corresponding grammar lesson discusses the pattern Noun + Intransitive Verb + Adverb (-ly).[3] Yet no examples of the pattern appear in any of the six reading passages.[4]

Part One, *Reading for Adult Beginners*, contains a list of words, the reading passage, and questions about the passage. The readings show no awareness of structural gradation, the first selection containing as many complex sentence patterns as the tenth. The reading passage includes such topics as "In the Cornfield," "A House on Fire," "A Workshop," "Riding a Horse," "The Blacksmith," "The Post Office," "The Diver," "Trade Unions," and "Mercury." Some topics contain useful information. Others, like the lesson on deep-sea diving, have no practical value.

The presentation in Part Two, *Lessons in Language*, is reminiscent of many late-nineteenth-century texts for native speakers. For example, a lesson on "The Statement" contains several illustrative sentences: *The river is frozen*; *Winter is gone*; *The robins have come*. The student is then confronted with such bewildering questions as "Of what does the first sentence tell something? What is told about it? Of what does the second sentence tell something? ... What does the third sentence tell?"[5] Such an approach, talking about language, offers little in establishing habits necessary for the mastery of grammatical structures.

Sarah O'Brien's text, *English for Foreigners*, stresses the need for pictures and other realia at all stages, especially for beginning students. Beginners should be given "objective" work—topics with concrete, demonstrable subjects. "As lessons advance from simple and concrete to more abstract ideas, the need for objective work diminishes in proportion to the pupils' growing mastery of the language."[6] The author regards the main object of language learning as building vocabulary, and to this end suggests the following procedure:

1. The teacher indicates the main idea, for example, nouns and articles, by pointing to himself and members of the class and pronouncing the words *man, woman*. The class repeats the words, in concert, then individually. The teacher does the same thing with *a man, a woman*.

2. The teacher writes the words on the blackboard, reads them, and the class repeats.

3. The teacher reads from the book and the students copy.[7]

Though noting that "the making of sentences goes hand and hand with the process of gaining vocabulary,"[8] the author makes few provisions for sentence drills, convinced instead that facility in sentence structure is acquired by frequent repetition of complete sentences. O'Brien stresses the fact that English pronunciation is exceedingly difficult for foreigners and provides drills on isolated sound problems by pronouncing individual words. However, there is no drill on reduced and sandhi forms, so that words like *an*, instead of containing an unstressed / ∂ /, are rhymed with *ban* and *hand*. Contractions are practiced only in writing, where they are not needed, but not in speech, where they are needed. The author follows a Gouin-like approach, which tends to ignore the separation of individual grammar patterns. Out of 148 lessons in the first book, less than half a dozen are built around a specific grammar pattern. According to the author, Book One provides a working knowledge of written English,[9] a highly dubious claim considering the lack of structural drill.

Book Two, though based on reading, is sounder linguistically. The lessons begin with a reading passage and topics on history, local government, health, education, and vocational guidance. Drawing examples from a passage, the teacher points out sentences in the past tense of the passive voice as another way of expressing past time, calling attention to the three endings / -t, -d, -n /. "These forms should be drilled upon in sentences, using also the auxiliary verbs *was, were*."[10] In this way, Book Two covers a considerable number of grammar patterns, presenting them inductively.

Anna Prior and Anna I. Ryan, in *How to Learn English*, emphasize that material should correspond to the experience and thought process of the foreigner. But their rendering of natural utterances seems rather odd: "I can see a ship. The ship is large. I can see men. I can see women. I can see boys. . . . I can see the ocean. These people have crossed the ocean in the ship. . . . One man comes from Greece. . . . I come from Russia. These men, women, boys, and girls are in America now."[11]

The lessons contain three parts: a list of vocabulary words, a reading passage, and questions. The questions are followed by partial answers with blanks to be filled in and are of two kinds, for example:

a. Where did you walk?
b. We ——— through the station.

a. Where was the writer born?
b. He was born in ———. (Answer to be found in the reading passage.)

The design of the questions with blanks often in the middle of the sentence makes them ill-suited to oral-aural work. With beginners, two weeks should be spent on "phonetic drills and on conversation about the immediate surroundings,"[12] but no specific directions are given for phonetic drills or on how to structure the conversation. The lessons contain no orderly presentation of structure; grammar patterns appear at random, often several at a time. The focus is actually on vocabulary, a fact stated in the introduction: "What we should give them is not sentences to pronounce, but a vocabulary to use in speaking."[13] The authors fail to realize that vocabulary words are of little use without the grammatical patterns that bind them together.

Like O'Brien's first volume, Houghton's *First Lessons in English for Foreigners in Evening Schools* rarely uses a grammar pattern as the basis for lessons. But unlike previous texts, it places greater emphasis on the oral approach in developing mastery:

Proficiency in English can be attained only through the constant use of English speech. To learn to speak and understand English a pupil must hear English spoken. It is necessary, therefore, that the teacher use over and over again, in every possible combination, every new word in each lesson; and in order that every pupil may use the words the greatest number of times possible, it is recommended that these oral exercises take the form of questions which will require the use in answers of these words in complete statements.[14]

To achieve the desired end, the author offers several drills:

1. Reading and Action Lesson for Two Pupils
   a. The lesson is presented first by the teacher as an oral exercise. The teacher asks questions and the student answers.
   b. Then the students open their books; one student reads the same question and another student reads the answer.
   c. A variation is the reading and action drill, which follows the same procedure, except that instead of a question, the first person issues a command, and the second one carries it out.
2. Reading and Action Lesson for Four Pupils
   a. It is first presented as an oral lesson in which the teacher gives the orders and asks the questions.
   b. Then in the reading, one pupil gives the order, one performs the action, one asks the question, and one gives the answer.

An example appears in Lesson 17:

PUPIL 1: Stand near your desk.
PUPIL 3: What is he doing?
PUPIL 4: He is standing near his desk.

Even the written lesson contains an oral stimulus. In Lesson 38, the teacher asks questions and the students write down the answers: "Write in your book the answers to these questions: Where were you born? When did you come to the United States? On what steamship did you come?"[15]

Another desirable feature combines the oral approach with the reading passage (Lesson 39). The lesson begins with a list of vocabulary words, followed by a Reading Lesson for Two Pupils which contains questions and answers later to appear in the straight reading lesson: "What weather do we have in the summer? In summer we have hot weather. . . . In what months do farmers plant their vegetables? In April and May." This is followed by the reading lesson which discusses similar material—seasons and weather in different parts of the country, planting, and other topics. In a second volume, Houghton follows the same approach but makes individual grammatical patterns the center of far more lessons.[16]

Ruth Austin's volume, *Lessons in English for Foreign Women*, suggests that the teacher use "all kinds of games to give variety and the social element needed to make the lesson interesting."[17] There seems little awareness of the need for controlled oral response: "Any desire which will lead to self-expression on the part of the pupils helps to give them a command of the English language."[18] In presenting the text material, the teacher is directed to explain the subject of the lesson carefully to the class but not to allow textbooks open until the lesson has been memorized. A typical lesson (Lesson 2) includes:

1. A group of sentences: "I get the breakfast for the family. We eat our breakfast. It is seven o'clock. I get ready to go to work. I put up my lunch." The class repeats the entire lesson until it is committed to memory. The text is then opened and the lesson is read aloud several times by the class; if the class is small enough, each student reads the entire lesson.

2. Memory exercise, used as an oral drill and as a writing exercise for homework, for example: "Who gets breakfast for the family? Who eats the breakfast? What time is it? What do I get ready to do? Do I put up my lunch?"

The book contains no reference to grammar patterns. While some

subject matter is of practical use, the author also presents such inanities as "I have one head," with corresponding questions in the memory exercise: "How many heads do I have?"[19]

Azniv Beshgeturian's text, *Foreigners' Guide to English*, builds most lessons around a grammar pattern and a few around such subjects as parts of the house, members of the family, weather, occupations, and seasons. Throughout the book, especially at the beginning, the author relies heavily on pictures. In addition, lessons include a list of vocabulary words at the beginning and several columns of words at the end for "phonic" drill. However, the words are supposed to be pronounced in isolation, and there is no use of reduced forms.

Some lessons include action questions within the pattern—for example, a lesson on the auxiliary *can*: "Can you write? Yes, I can write. Write your name. Write mine on this paper. Write hers on that paper."[20] Several lessons begin with a complete paradigm of a verb form: "I have worked. You have worked. He . . . She . . . We . . . They . . . ."[21] There are no specific directions for teaching the elements of the paradigm. Presumably a fair amount of time is spent on memorizing elements orally in class. The author also uses pictures with related questions to elicit a written response. For example, in Lesson 18 a man is pictured sitting in a chair reading, and below are directions to answer the following questions: "Is this man standing? . . . Where is the man sitting? . . . What has he in his hand?"

The most active figure in EFL during the 1920's was Henry H. Goldberger, whose work is examined in Chapter III. In addition to teaching EFL methods at Teachers College, Columbia, he wrote one book and several manuals on EFL methodology, plus two texts for foreign students. The first text, *English for Coming Citizens*, emphasizes oral mastery as the main goal: "The foreigner in this country has . . . a greater need for knowing how to speak English than he has for knowing how to read, and he has a far greater need for knowing how to read than he has for knowing how to write."[22] Clearly recognizing the need for teaching linguistic forms in context, he states: "We cannot teach foreigners conjugations, declensions, and isolated words, and expect them to know anything else but conjugations, declensions, and isolated words."[23] Regarding methodology, he explains: "Since language is learned primarily through the ear, the subject-matter of a text must in all cases be developed orally by means of dramatizations and of objects."[24]

Each chapter consists of two parts: the text and exercises based on it. Only when the meaning of a lesson has been demonstrated by the teacher do the students open their books:

> Now the eye is called upon to help out the ear. The teacher once more performs the acts and reads the sentences in the book. The pupils are . . . called upon to perform the act and at the same time to read the sentences in the book. Thus a double association will be established between the ideas, the spoken words, and the printed words.[25]

Chapters are organized by subjects of everyday experience such as "Buying Shoes," "Renting a Flat," "Ordering Goods by Mail." As in the other books examined here, very few lessons are arranged by grammatical pattern. Of 117 chapters, only 17 are built around a single structure, for example, present perfect tense, relative pronouns, and prepositions. A conversation in Lesson 57 contains "We *shall* be glad to exchange them if they *do not* fit"; but "I'll take them."

Though many grammar patterns are used, they are not presented systematically, and the book shows no awareness of the need for repeating newly presented patterns. Chapters are divided into a beginning story, exercises, and parts called conversation or questions. Simple present and imperative forms are used frequently from the start and throughout the book. A tabulation of the first fifty chapters of the book reveals a highly limited number of patterns: twenty-seven plus *can*, the imperative, simple present, continuous present, and comparison of adjectives, for a total of thirty-two. Of these, nine appear only once, and such important forms as the simple future only eleven times.

Goldberger's other text, a reader entitled *Second Book in English for Coming Citizens*, stresses that oral reading contributes little in language learning. Instead, lessons should be presented in the following way:

1. The teacher introduces the subject matter by asking questions.
2. The teacher selects a number of words and phrases from the text, uses them in other contexts, and writes them on the board.
3. The author suggests a host of drills to facilitate word recognition and the use of unfamiliar structures.
4. The teacher reads the chapter aloud.
5. Students then read the chapter silently.
6. To stimulate the students' self-expression, the teacher asks questions at the end of the chapter.

Our final volume is *English for Coming Americans. Advanced Course* by Peter Roberts. Lessons are divided into a story and language lessons. The lessons include word study—different form classes of words from the story, for example, school-schooling-scholar—homonyms, and grammatical explanation of some part of speech, capitalization, and so forth. The story is laid out in the following way:

1492:	Christopher Columbus found America in 1492.
born:	He was born in Genoa, Italy, in 1445.
parents:	His parents were poor and gave him little schooling.
sailor:	He became a sailor when he was 14 years old.
flat:	He believed the earth was flat.
married:	He was a good sailor and married a sailor's daughter.
maps:	His wife gave him some maps and charts.[26]

APPENDIX 2: *Analysis of Early EFL Texts*

The teacher writes key words on the board, and students form sentences from them without looking at the book. If necessary, the teacher asks questions to help students use the right word. He then points to a picture of Columbus and a map of the United States, explaining "He found America." Afterward the teacher writes *1492* on the blackboard and the lesson proceeds:

TCHR: Christopher Columbus found America in 1492.
CLASS: Christopher Columbus found America in 1492.
TCHR: What took place in 1492?
CLASS: Christopher Columbus found America.
TCHR: What did Columbus do?
CLASS: He found America in 1492.[27]

The same procedure is followed throughout the story. In presenting different form classes in the word-study section, the teacher asks a student to form a sentence with the word *school* and write it on the board. Then the teacher asks, "What did Columbus' parents give him?" The student replies, "They gave him little schooling."

The grammar section never goes beyond an intellectual explanation of grammatical phenomena. Chapter One, for example, comments on nouns and verbs: "The names of persons and things, as *Columbus, ship, port,* are called nouns. . . . The words which tell what the persons and things are doing, or that they exist, as, Columbus *came* to Lisbon, the ship *sails,* the port *is* large, are called verbs."[28]

The textbooks examined in this section show a fairly wide range of approaches to language teaching. In contrast to modern EFL texts, these older volumes pay little attention to the central importance of grammar patterns, mixing them indiscriminately. Goldberger's first volume, which is typical, omits regular repetition of structures for the purpose of reinforcing learning. Moreover, the kind of language taught was not completely natural, as shown by the rhyming of *an* with *ban, hand, bank* in O'Brien, and by the lack of reduced forms or contractions in O'Brien, Beshgeturian, and Goldberger.

Appendix 3. Statistics on Foreign Students in the United States

Number of Foreign Students, by Year, in American Universities and Colleges

Year	Number	Year	Number	Year	Number
1911:	3,645	1932:	6,850	1948:	25,464
1913:	4,222[a]	1934:	5,860[d]	1949:	26,433[f]
1919:	7,000[b]	1935:	5,608	1953:	33,675[g]
1921:	6,488[c]	1937:	7,343	1954:	34,200[h]
1922:	7,494	1938:	6,064[e]	1955:	34,232
1923:	6,988	1939:	6,670	1958:	43,391
1925:	6,981	1940:	7,152	1961:	53,107
1926:	7,541	1942:	8,056	1962:	58,000[i]
1928:	9,685	1944:	7,542	1963:	64,705
1929:	10,033	1945:	10,341	1964:	82,000
1930:	4,961	1946:	16,176	1965:	93,000[j]
1931:	8,688	1947:	18,631	1970:	100,000 (est.)[k]

[a] Samuel Capen, *Opportunities for Foreign Students at Colleges and Universities in the United States*, 57.

[b] Martena Tenney Sasnett (ed.), *A Guide to the Admission and Placement of Foreign Students*, forward.

[c] Institute of International Education, *Annual Report of the Director* (1933), 64.

[d] Institute of International Education, *Annual Report* (1937), 51.

Foreign Students, Countries of Origin, 1914

Country	Number
Canada	653
China	594
Japan	336
Great Britain and Ireland	223
Cuba	212
India	209
Finland	162
Germany	124
Brazil	122
Argentina	113

SOURCE: Capen, *Opportunities for Foreign Students at Colleges and Universities in the United States*, 58.

Foreign Students' Fields of Specialization, 1914

Field	Number
Undergraduate Arts and Sciences	1,700
Engineering	801
Medicine	339
Dentistry	303
Agriculture	275
Theology	256
Commerce and Business Administration	95

[e] Institute of International Education, *Annual Report* (1949), 133.

[f] Institute of International Education, *Education for One World,* 58.

[g] Institute of International Education, *Educational Exchange in the Atlantic Area,* 30.

[h] Institute of International Education, *Open Doors 1965,* 4.

[i] Committee on Educational Interchange Policy, *A Foreign Student Program for the Developing Countries During the Coming Decades,* 2.

[j] Institute of International Education, *Open Doors 1965,* 4.

[k] *Ibid.,* 2.

Colleges with the Greatest Number of Foreign Students, Selected Years

School	No.	School	No.	School	No.
		1926[a]			
U. California	376	Harvard	380	Cornell	197
Yale	139	M.I.T.	208	N.Y.U.	138
U. Chicago	309	U. Michigan	248	U. Pennsylvania	216
U. Illinois	117	Columbia	895	U. Washington	270
		1929[b]			
Stanford	116	Harvard	256	Cornell	171
U. California	593	M.I.T.	203	N.Y.U.	626
Lewis Institute	141	U. Michigan	264	Syracuse	189
Northwestern	126	U. Minnesota	268	U. Pennsylvania	209
U. Chicago	275	St. Louis U.	120	U. Washington	264
U. Illinois	169	Columbia	710	U. Wisconsin	113
Johns Hopkins	114				
		1932[c]			
U. California	563	Harvard	134	N.Y.U.	405
U.C.L.A.	136	U. Michigan	274	U. Pennsylvania	108
U. Chicago	233	Columbia	346	U. Washington	130
U. Illinois	164	Cornell	171		
		1936[d]			
U. California	639	M.I.T.	212	Cornell	177
U.C.L.A.	211	U. Michigan	244	U. Pennsylvania	123
U. S. Cal.	285	U. Minnesota	137	U. Washington	397
U. Chicago	141	Columbia	399		
		1940[e]			
U. California	461	M.I.T.	170	Cornell	194
U.C.L.A.	180	U. Michigan	254	N.Y.U.	328
U. Chicago	152	Columbia	494	U. Washington	222
Harvard	259				

School	No.	School	No.	School	No.
		1943[f]			
U. California	288	M.I.T.	225	Teachers College	174
U.C.L.A.	167	U. Michigan	303	Cornell	132
Harvard	272	Columbia	359	U. Texas	111
		1946[g]			
U. California	844	U. Illinois	176	Teachers College	350
U. S. Cal.	162	L.S.U.	274	N.Y.U.	355
Yale	198	Harvard	613	U. Pennsylvania	160
Howard U.	187	M.I.T.	290	U. Texas	185
U. Chicago	202	U. Michigan	457	U. Washington	221
Columbia	989	U. Minnesota	311		
		1951[h]			
U. California	1,459	U. Washington	449	U. Pennsylvania	296
Columbia	1,379	U. Wisconsin	423	Stanford	271
N.Y.U.	1,185	U. Illinois	417	Michigan State	247
U. Michigan	781	Cornell	400	Yale	247
Harvard	730	U. Chicago	355	Ohio State	213
U. Minnesota	512	U. S. Cal.	303	Howard U.	212
M.I.T.	493	U. Texas	303		
		1964[i]			
U. California	4,393	Michigan State	854	U. Texas	530
N.Y.U.	2,986	Indiana U.	809	U. Kansas	526
Columbia	2,353	U. Hawaii	757	Oklahoma State	510
U. Wisconsin	1,377	U. Washington	739	Kansas St.	487
U. Minnesota	1,367	Stanford	709	U. Arizona	485
Howard U.	1,258	Purdue	690	L.S.U.	484
U. Illinois	1,243	U. Missouri	666	Catholic U.	462
U. Penn.	1,232	Yale	652	Iowa State	453
U. Michigan	1,181	Ohio State	627	U. Florida	438
Harvard	1,054	U. N. Carolina	601	Calif. State Poly.	428
Wayne State	1,013	Brigham Young	592	San Francisco St.	420

School	No.	School	No.	School	No.
Cornell	1,008	U. Oregon	550	U. Oklahoma	415
U. S. Cal.	1,007	Syracuse	534	Utah State	414
M.I.T.	915	U. Chicago	533	Texas A & M	403

[a] Institute of International Education, *Annual Report of the Director* (1927), 35-37.

[b] Institute of International Education, *Annual Report* (1929-31), 44-47.

[c] Institute of International Education, *Annual Report* (1933), 65-67.

[d] Institute of International Education, *Annual Report* (1935-37), 52-55.

[e] Institute of International Education, *Annual Report* (1941), 42-46.

[f] Institute of International Education, *Annual Report* (1944), 67-71.

[g] Institute of International Education, *Annual Report* (1947), 100-109.

[h] DuBois, *Foreign Students and Higher Education in the United States,* 201.

[i] Institute of International Education, *Open Doors 1965,* 7.

Appendix 4. Illustrative Grammar Lessons

Pattern: 1. Review of *before* and *after*
2. Two-word verbs: *pick up, put down, turn on, turn off, hang up, turn up, turn down, put on, take off*

A. Teacher asks questions, and students answer. All three positions are taught.
   1. pick up, put down (book, gloves, etc.)
      a. What did I do?   (You picked up the book.)
                                   (You picked the book up.)
                                   (You picked it up.)
      b. What did I do?   (You put the book down.)
      Am I picking it up or putting it down?
   2. put on, take off (coat, gloves, earrings, etc.)
      What did I do?   (You put on your coat.)
      What did I just do?   (You just took it off.)
      Am I putting it on or taking it off?
   3. hang up (coat, scarf)
      What did I just do?   (You just hung up your coat.)
   4. turn on, turn off (lights, model of a radio, etc.)
      What am I doing?   (You're turning off the lights.)

What did I just do?   (You just turned on the lights.)
Did I turn them on or off?
5. turn up, turn down (model of a radio)
What am I doing?   (You're turning the radio up.)
It's too loud.
What did I just do?   (You just turned it down.)

B. In reading the story, the teacher interrupts at the indicated places and asks questions:

Story	*Questions*
Mr. Baxter's son came home from school one day. He didn't want to do his homework./	Did he want to do his homework? What didn't he want to do?/
He took off his coat, but he didn't hang it up.	What did he do with his coat? What didn't he do?/
He took his shoes off./	What did he do with his shoes? When did he take them off? What did he do before he took off his shoes?/
He picked up a newspaper, but he didn't want to read it./	What did he do after he took off his shoes? What did he do before he picked up the newspaper? Did he want to read the newspaper? What did he do with it?/
He put it down. Then he picked up a magazine. He looked at it for five minutes. Then he put it down./	Then what did he do? When did he pick up the magazine? How long did he read it? What did he do with it?
He turned on the radio./	What did he do after he put down the magazine? What did he do before he turned on the radio? When did he turn it on?/
There was an opera on, but he	What was playing? Did he

Story	Questions
didn't want to listen to it, so he turned it off./	want to listen to it? What did he do?/
He turned on the TV. It was a good cowboy program./	What did he do after he turned off the radio? When did he turn on the TV?/
But he couldn't hear it. It wasn't loud enough, so he turned it up. Then it was too loud, so he turned it down./	Was it loud enough? What did he do with the TV set? Why? Then what did he do?
Finally, he turned it off, put on his shoes, and left./	

At this point the students should be able to retell the story by themselves, individually or consecutively. The teacher calls on individual students one after another: What did he do after he came home? What did he do after he took off his coat? When did he take off his shoes? And so on. It can then be worked backwards: What did he do before he turned off the TV set? What did he do before he turned it down?

LESSON 2

Pattern: Verb + -ing form as a noun (I *finished studying* at 12 o'clock). This pattern may be used with *avoid, can't help, consider, dislike, depend on, enjoy, finish, insist on, imagine, practice, risk, stop, suggest, (try), (begin)*. The last two also take the infinitive form.

A. This story is a continuation of another one from a previous lesson that contains a different pattern.

Story	Questions
Mr. Smith enjoyed fishing in Florida, but he couldn't help	What did Mr. Smith enjoy doing? Where? What couldn't

Story

thinking about the fish that got away./

He decided that he would practice casting with an inexpensive rod./

Then he would consider buying an expensive one and going back to Florida./

When he finished practicing, he returned to Florida./

Mr. Smith insisted on taking the same boat, and soon he was out in the ocean again./

He threw in his line, but he avoided keeping it too tight./

He wasn't nervous this time. He enjoyed sitting back in the chair and relaxing./

After a while, he even stopped thinking about fishing. He was more interested in enjoying the sun and the breeze./

In fact, he couldn't help dozing off occasionally./

While he was dozing, he imagined catching a great big fish./

Suddenly, he woke up. Something was pulling on his line. He tried holding the line tight./

He tried pulling in the line quickly,/

but the thing at the other end gave a sharp pull, and Mr. Smith found himself in the water. After that, he decided that he would go skiing on his next vacation./

Questions

he help doing?/

What did he decide to do?/

Then what would he consider doing? When? Where would he consider going?/

When did he return to Florida? What did he do when he finished practicing?/

What did he insist on doing?

What did he do with his line? What did he avoid doing?/

Did he feel nervous? How did he feel? What did he enjoy doing?/

What did he stop doing? What was he more interested in?/

What couldn't he help doing?/ What did he imagine doing? When?/

Why did Mr. Smith wake up suddenly? What did he try doing?/

What else did he try doing?/

What did the fish do? What did he decide after that? Why?/

B. Using the same verbs, the teacher asks questions about the students:
1. What kind of things do you enjoy doing?
2. What kind of things do you dislike doing?
3. When I was a child, I imagined being an explorer. What kind of person did you imagine being?
4. Do you mind writing letters to friends? What things don't you mind doing?
5. What kind of things do you avoid doing when you travel?
6. At what age do you hope to stop working?
7. What do you insist on having when you go to a good restaurant?
8. When people get married, the wife does certain things and the husband does certain things. (If married) what kind of things do you insist on doing?
9. Certain things are necessary for the successful operation of a modern corporation. What are some of the things that a manufacturing company depends on? (It depends on selling its products. It depends on getting enough raw materials.)

Appendix 5. Trends in EFL Teaching in the 1950's and 1960's

CURRENT PROGRAMS and courses in EFL range from two to thirty-five hours a week. Such a range allows for considerable difference in composition. Some programs utilize the language laboratory; others do not. The way individual skills (speaking, listening, reading, and writing) are arranged into courses also shows great diversity. Such elements as the number of levels and the number of hours per week show variation as well. Six studies conducted between 1956 and 1967 present different aspects of contemporary EFL programs. And though these studies do not all focus on the same elements or use the same sampling techniques, we can derive from them a composite picture of the EFL program in its development over the last twenty years.

The 1956 NAFSA study by David P. Harris was a survey of intermediate-level EFL programs in 20 colleges.[1] The survey was restricted to courses for students who already had at least elementary knowledge of the English language but were not proficient enough to be admitted as regular students. The study excluded English language institutes with courses for students at the beginning level. A 1961 State Department survey (published by NAFSA) included a much wider sampling (952 institutions of higher learning) and examined in greater depth the English language programs and needs of colleges and universities at all levels of language proficiency.[2] A 1963 report by the Institute of International Education covered 180 institutions and provides such information as the various levels offered, the number of hours per week, and, in some cases, a listing of specific courses.[3] Similarly, the 1966 report by the Center for Applied Linguistics (CAL), covering 150 institutions, contains information on course levels and hours per week.[4] A study done for the NCTE under the direction of Harold B. Allen, published in 1966, attempts to describe every aspect of the EFL program at all educational levels. The survey, based on 510 replies, covers the period from April, 1964, to March, 1966.[5] A survey dealing with the academic year 1965–66 examines intermediate and advanced level programs in EFL and contains information based on 54 replies.[6] Prepared for the Association of Teachers of English as a Second Language, the survey includes questions on the language laboratory, average class size, and elements of the English language emphasized in the course. The 1956, 1961, 1966 (NCTE), and 1967 (NAFSA) studies all include information on the most widely used textbooks.

Table 1: Number of Semesters, per cent

Year	1	2	3	4
1956	30 (6)[a]	45 (9)	15 (3)	—
1961 (small schools)[b]	44	45.5	4	1.5 (11)
(large schools)	40.5	36	11.5	4 (19)

[a] Figures in parentheses stand for actual numbers of schools.

[b] Small schools are those with no more than 30 foreign students (766 schools), while large schools are those with more than 30 (186 schools).

It is difficult to draw conclusions from the limited 1956 sampling of 20 colleges. However, it does agree with the 1961 survey, which shows the largest percentage of schools with two semesters in their EFL course. The 1956 survey, concerned only with the intermediate level, points out that 30 per cent of the intermediate courses were only one semester long. The 1966 NCTE material is divided by months and is therefore not suitable for comparison. Unless the EFL program includes other levels (see Table 2), two semesters do not seem enough time to provide the student sufficient training for carrying on university-level work. However, an evaluation must take into account the number of hours, which among 18 institutions averaged five a week. The average class size in the 1956 survey was 19.8 students. In the 1966 NCTE survey, 49.7 per cent of classes had 11 to 20 students, with 37.5 per cent below and 12.7 per cent above that figure, while the 1967 NAFSA survey of 54 institutions showed a class average of 10 to 15 students.

The most noticeable trend is the continued expansion in the number of levels offered and a drop in the number of institutions offering only one level. The number of schools with three levels rose from 10 per cent (12.5 per cent)[7] in 1961 to 36 per cent in 1966. The percentage of schools offering two levels rose from 8 per cent (18 per cent) in 1961 to 28.6 per cent in 1966, while the percentage of schools offering only one level dropped from 29 per cent (39 per cent) to 22 per cent of their respective universes.

Table 2: Number of Levels, per cent

Year	1	2	3	4	4–6	8–9
1961 (small schools)[a]	29	8	10	—	—	—
(large schools)	39	18	12.5	2(3)[b]		
1963[c]	16.6	19.4	19.4	—[d]	——	——
1966 (CAL)[c]	22	28.6	36	4.6	1.3	1.3
				(7 programs)	(2 programs)	(2 programs)

[a] In 53 per cent of the small schools and 28.5 per cent of the large ones, students were not separated by proficiency level.

[b] Figures in parentheses stand for actual number of schools.

[c] In some cases, the level is not indicated.

[d] Not specified.

Table 3: Hours per Week, per cent

Year	1	2	3	4	5	6	8	10	Over 10	11–19	20 & over
1956	none	none	12.5 (2)[a]	6 (1)	62.5 (10)	6 (1)	none (1)	6	none	none	none
1961 (small schools)	2.5	17	31.5	9	16	2.5	none	2	9 (68.9)	none	none
(large schools)	none	7.5	35	5.5	15.5	3	2	4	9 (16.7)	none	none
1966 (CAL)[b]	1.3 (2)	7.3 (11)	35 (53)	10.6 (16)	22 (33)	10 (15)	4 (6)	3.3 (5)	29 (38)	11 (17)	18 (27)
1966 (NCTE)[c]	2.4	14.7	17.6	8.8	21.6	[d]					

[a] Figures in parentheses stand for actual number of schools.
[b] The same school may, for example, have a beginning course of six hours, an intermediate course of four hours, and an advanced course of three. This accounts for the fact that the 1966 total is over 100 per cent.
[c] The 1966 NCTE survey can be most readily compared with the 1961 small college report, since both are based on universes of over 500 each. Accordingly, the 1966 survey includes a greater number of "small college" respondents than does the 1966 CAL study.
[d] Lists six or more as 9.4 per cent.

Since most EFL programs are to a certain extent self-supporting, this greater delineation of courses is made possible largely by increased student enrollment; the more students, the greater the opportunity for courses at different levels of proficiency.

Since the 1966 CAL study covers schools with 50 or more foreign students, its sample is closer to the large school entry in the 1961 survey (size of the sample was 186 for 1961 and 150 for 1966). Thus, the 1961 large school figures seem more valid for purposes of comparison with the 1966 study. Significantly, only two schools still offer courses that meet but once a week. There is little appreciable change in the number of courses meeting two, three, eight, or ten times a week, a slight increase in courses meeting four and five hours per week, and a fairly marked rise in those meeting six hours per week.

The greatest increase is shown in the number of courses meeting more than ten hours. Thus, with the expanding number of levels, there has been a general trend toward courses with more time per week. The most common course remains one that meets three hours per week.

Table 4: Hours per Week
(1966 CAL survey)

Elementary	Intermediate	Advanced
5 hrs./week (15)[a]	3 hrs./week (31)	3 hrs./week (32)
3 hrs./week (14)	5 hrs./week (27)	5 hrs./week (17)
20 hrs./week (8)	6 hrs./week (10)	4 hrs./week (11)
25 hrs./week (8)	20 hrs./week (8)	6 hrs./week (8)
	25 hrs./week (8)	25 hrs./week (8)

[a] Figures in parentheses refer to number of institutions.

Further analysis of the 1966 CAL study reveals that the most common number of hours per week for the beginning course is five, followed by three hours per week. The situation is reversed at the intermediate and advanced levels, both showing three and five hours as the first and second most common time allotments (Table 4).

Table 5: Course Content, per cent

Subject	Large Schools	Small Schools
Speaking	26.4	24.2
Reading	21.6	24.4
Writing	32.7	28.4
Grammar	19.2	23.0

In the 1961 survey, a total of 90 small and 69 large schools answered questions on the general content of their courses. Analysis of these figures shows that writing received the most time in both small school and large school programs (among the four areas of speaking, reading, writing, and grammar). This is significant in light of the fact that linguists tend to place writing near the bottom in importance of language skills to be taught. Among large schools, speaking is second in importance, followed by reading, whereas speaking and reading receive approximately equal emphasis in the small schools.

An element of uncertainty enters into this aspect of the 1961 survey from its use of the terms *speaking* and *grammar*. In a sense, these terms represent two separate categories. There is perennial concern in foreign language programs over the amount of time to be spent on the different "skills": reading, writing, vocabulary, pronunciation. However, a distinction is rarely made between skills, and language elements. The skills include reading, writing, speaking, and listening, while the language elements include grammar, vocabulary, and pronunciation. The skills may be regarded as different ways of teaching the language elements, or certain language elements can be regarded as components of different skills. All four skills can be used in the teaching of grammar and vocabulary, while only speaking and listening can be used in teaching pronunciation. The relationships in both directions can be seen in the diagram below:

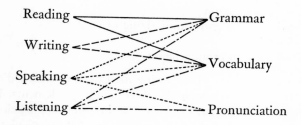

It has become axiomatic that the oral-aural approach (speaking-listening) is the chief method in EFL teaching today. However, this assumption has not been proven. An analysis and tabulation of certain elements in the 1967 survey enable us to examine this thesis. These findings, it must be remembered, apply only to intermediate and advanced courses. However, there are certain similarities to the 1961 study. The 1967 NAFSA survey reveals the percentage of respondents that emphasized the following areas and procedures:

Areas	*Per cent*
1. Oral-aural drill in controlled patterns of syntax and morphology	83
2. Oral-aural vocabulary drill	75
3. Written drill on syntactic patterns	75
4. Controlled paragraph writing	83
5. Free written composition	79
6. Composition based on reading selections	51
7. Reading comprehension activities	81
8. Dictation practice in language patterns	72

This list can be used to determine the extent to which different skills are used in teaching the three language elements. In the paragraphs on grammar, vocabulary, and pronunciation below, the numbers in parentheses are an integral part of the particular activity. For example, in number 12, free conversation, all three elements of grammar, vocabulary, and pronunciation would be practiced, whereas number 4, controlled writing, involves learning and practice only in grammar and vocabulary.

The kinds of exercises that contain work on grammatical structures are numbers 1, 3, 8, 10, (4), (5), (6), (7), (9), (11), (12), and (13). Analysis of these items shows the percentages of time that different skills are used in the teaching of grammar:

Skill	*Per cent of Time*
Speaking	14.0
Speaking-Listening	10.4
Listening	8.4
Listening-Writing	14.0
Writing	36.0
Reading	17.4

Speaking occupies only 14 per cent of the time in teaching grammar—the same amount of time as listening-writing and less than reading or writing. Even combined with speaking-listening, the oral-aural approach is used only 24.4 per cent of the time, as opposed to writing, which is used for 36 per cent of the time in teaching grammar. At the intermediate and advanced levels, where command of the basic patterns has been achieved, increasing emphasis on reading and writing is understandable. However, the 1961 survey (Table 5), which covers all levels, also reveals a heavy emphasis on writing.

The kinds of exercises that contain vocabulary practice are numbers 2, (5), (6), (7), and (9). Analysis of these items shows the percentage of time different skills are used in the teaching of vocabulary:

Skill	Per cent of Time
Speaking	0.0
Speaking-Listening	17.0
Listening	15.4
Listening-Writing	0.0
Writing	48.8
Reading	18.8

The most striking fact here is that the oral-aural method is used far less (17 per cent) than writing (48.8 per cent) for the teaching and practice of vocabulary.

The kinds of exercises that contain pronunciation practice are numbers 14, (12), and (13). Analysis of these items shows that learning and practice of pronunciation are done by speaking (54.6 per cent) and speaking-listening (45.4 per cent).

It is difficult to measure these conclusions against the comprehensive 1966 NCTE survey, which in questions addressed to institutions found that the following were emphasized by the highest percentage of colleges: written composition, 58.1 per cent; writing, 58.1 per cent; reading 56.3 per cent; pronunciation, 55.9 per cent; and speaking fluency, 53.7 per cent. Moreover, in the same survey of institutions, 55.5 per cent reported use of the oral-aural or audio-lingual method; 41.5 per cent reported using the

Textbooks Used in EFL Courses

Textbook	1956	1961 5 or more	1966 NCTE	1967
Baumwell and Saitz, *Advanced Reading and Writing*	–	–	–	5
Bigelow and Harris, *The United States*	–	×	–	4
Croft, *Reading and Word Study*	–	×	18	4
Danielson and Hayden, *Reading in English*	–	–	10	5
Dixson series	2	×	–	–
Doty and Ross, *Language and Life in the United States*	–	×	19	4
Fries–Lado series	6	×	15	15
Hayden, Haggard, and Pilgrim, *Mastering American English*	–	×	26	8
Kaplan, *Reading and Rhetoric*	–	–	–	4
Newmark, Hinely, and Mintz, *Using American English*	–	–	–	4
Paratore, *English Exercises*	–	×	6	–
Praninskas, *Rapid Review of English Grammar*	–	–	30	10
Prator, *Manual of American English Pronunciation*	2	×	7	–
Ross and Doty, *Writing English*	–	–	–	8
Taylor, *American English Reader*	–	×	5	–
Taylor, *Learning American English*	2	×	13	–
Taylor, *Mastering American English*	–	×	7	–
Wright, *Practice Your English*	4	×	5	–

direct method; and 41.5 per cent also subscribed to what was called the linguistic or structural approach. However, the direct method need not be oral-aural. The term merely refers to the fact that all work is done in the foreign language. It says nothing about the method of presentation. Similarly, the principle of structural control can be followed with written or spoken material. The term is not confined to a specific language skill.

Discussion of current textbooks must take into account a limitation of the 1967 survey; it is an examination of intermediate and advanced level programs and as such does not contain information on texts used at the elementary level. Of the eleven most common books listed in the 1967 survey, six deal specifically with reading and writing. Three of the top six (books mentioned by five or more respondents) were concerned chiefly with reading and writing—Ross and Doty, Danielson and Hayden, and Baumwell and Saitz—while a fourth, Hayden, Haggard, and Pilgrim, also emphasizes writing but provides a small amount of oral-aural work. These figures tend to reinforce the observation made in the previous section that writing (and reading) is emphasized over oral-aural work. The second most popular text mentioned by respondents, Praninskas' *Rapid Review of English Grammar*, emphasizes the oral-aural approach but also makes some provision for written work. Most popular was the University of Michigan series (15 respondents), which leans even more heavily on the oral-aural approach in each of its four volumes.

The volumes devoted primarily to the teaching of grammar patterns include Fries–Lado, Taylor (*Learning American English, Mastering American English*); Wright; Paratore; Hayden, Haggard, and Pilgrim; Praninskas; and Newmark, Hinely, and Mintz. Of these, only Praninskas contains specific provisions for eliciting what might be called "contextual" material, that is, information based on the student's own background or the student's own point of view. Examples of the former include questions like the following, used in practicing the continuous present perfect tense plus *for*:

How long have you been living in the United States?
How long have you been attending this university?
How long have you been studying English?

Examples of material based on the student's own point of view include questions like the following, for practicing the pattern *by* + verb + *-ing*:

How do you learn a foreign language?
How can I keep up with current events?
How can I find out what's playing at the movies?

Taylor's texts *Learning American English* and *Mastering American English* chiefly contain substitution and conversion exercises. A great many of these, because of their design, are not of much use for oral-aural work, their main value being as homework exercises. Oral-aural exercises are those that the teacher can present to the students orally and which they can respond to without use of their books. In this respect, the grammar exercises in Paratore's *English Exercises*, Dixon's *Beginning Lessons*, and Hayden, Haggard, and Pilgrim's *Mastering American English* are best used for written work.

The surveys discussed here suggest a far lower acceptance of the oral-aural method than one might imagine. Skills such as reading and writing become increasingly important at the advanced level, as the formal demands of university life make themselves felt. But the elementary course, with its focus on speaking, listening, and pronunciation, clearly requires the oral-aural approach in order to achieve its goal.

This brief observation of EFL texts indicates considerable need for elementary grammar texts that utilize the oral-aural method *in contextual situations of sentence length and longer*.

Notes

II. The Historical Background of Linguistics and Language Teaching Before 1880

[1] William M. Smail, *Quintilian on Education*, viii.

[2] Aubrey Gwynn, *Roman Education from Cicero to Quintilian*, 190.

[3] Smail, *op. cit.*, 37.

[4] *Quintilian's Institutes of Oratory: or, the Education of an Orator* (trans. by John Selby Watson), I, 58.

[5] *Ibid.*, 64.

[6] John P. Hughes, *The Science of Language*, 48.

[7] Smail, *op. cit.*, xlv.

[8] William H. Woodward, *Desiderius Erasmus Concerning the Aim of Modern Education*, xvii.

[9] *Ibid.*, xviii.

[10] *Ibid.*, 108.

[11] *Ibid.*, 163–64.

[12] Palsgrave, *L'éclaircissement de la langue française*, 3.

[13] *Ibid.*, xvi.

[14] *Ibid.*, xxi.

[15] *Ibid.*

[16] Palsgrave, *op. cit.*, 418.

[17] S. S. Laurie, *John Amos Comenius*, 165.

[18] Will S. Monroe, *Comenius and the Beginnings of Educational Reform*, 126–27.

[19] *Ibid.*, 132.

[20] *Ibid.*, 136.

[21] Robert H. Quick, *Essays on Educational Reformers,* 140.

[22] Laurie, *op. cit.,* 91.

[23] George E. Ganss, *Saint Ignatius' Idea of a Jesuit University,* 218.

[24] *Ibid.,* 221.

[25] Marcel, *The Study of Languages,* 111.

[26] *Ibid.,* 22.

[27] *Ibid.,* 15.

[28] *Ibid.,* 43.

[29] *Ibid.,* 118.

[30] *Ibid.,* 117.

[31] R. H. Robins, *Ancient and Medieval Grammatical Theory,* 72.

[32] Robert Pooley, *Teaching English Grammar,* 14.

[33] Loughton, *Practical Grammar of the English Tongue.*

[34] Sterling Leonard, *Doctrines of Correctness in English Usage, 1700–1800,* 135.

[35] Paul Roberts, *Understanding English,* 382.

[36] Baugh, *op. cit.,* 340.

[37] James Sledd and Gwin J. Kolb, *Dr. Johnson's Dictionary,* 134.

[38] Baugh, *op. cit.,* 334.

[39] Leonard, *op. cit.,* 11.

[40] Pooley, *op. cit.,* 18.

[41] Priestly, *The Rudiments of English Grammar,* vi–vii.

[42] Rollo Lyman, *English Grammar in American Schools Before 1850,* 11.

[43] Priestly, *op. cit.,* ix.

[44] *Ibid.,* vii.

[45] *Ibid.,* xvii.

[46] Baugh, *op. cit.,* 341.

[47] *Ibid.,* 342.

[48] *Ibid.*

[49] Greene, *First Lessons in Grammar Based on the Construction and Analysis of Sentences,* 4.

[50] *Ibid.,* 4–5.

[51] *Ibid.,* 5.

[52] *Ibid.*

[53] *Ibid.,* 11.

[54] W. Nelson Francis, *The Structure of American English,* 128.

[55] Greene, *op. cit.,* 23.

[56] *Ibid.,* 24.

[57] *Ibid.,* 27–28. Cf. Kenneth Croft, *Reading and Word Study for Students*

of English as a Second Language, 315–21, and Grant Taylor, *American English Reader,* 128–29.

[58] Greene, *op. cit.,* 132.

[59] Greene, *A Treatise on the Structure of the English Language.*

[60] E. W. Bagster-Collins, *The History of Modern Language Teaching in the United States,* 89.

[61] Sauveur, *Introduction to the Teaching of Living Languages without Grammar or Dictionary,* 8.

[62] *Ibid.*

[63] *Ibid.,* 26.

[64] *Ibid.,* 19.

[65] *Ibid.,* 45.

III. *The Development of Linguistic and Language Teaching Theory in the United States, 1880–1940*

[1] H. A. Gleason, *Linguistics and English Grammar,* 20.

[2] Charles C. Fries, *Linguistics and Reading,* 55.

[3] Robert W. Albright, "The I.P.A.: Its Backgrounds and Development," *International Journal of American Linguistics,* Vol. XXIV, No. 1, Part 3 (1958), 2.

[4] Bror Danielsson, *John Hart's Works on English Orthography and Pronunciation,* 118.

[5] *Ibid.,* 119.

[6] *Ibid.,* 173–74.

[7] *Ibid.,* 247.

[8] *Ibid.*

[9] Albright, "The I.P.A.," *loc. cit.,* 7.

[10] *Ibid.*

[11] *Ibid.,* 8.

[12] *Ibid.,* 21.

[13] Bell, *Visible Speech,* 20.

[14] *Ibid.,* 17.

[15] *Ibid.,* 35.

[16] Sweet, *A Handbook of Phonetics,* vii.

[17] Albright, "The I.P.A.," *loc. cit.,* 53.

[18] Hughes, *op. cit.*

[19] Nicholai Trubetzkoy, "La phonologie actuelle," *Journal de Psychologie,* XXXe année, Nos. 1–4 (January 15–April 15, 1933), 229.

[20] Daniel Jones, "The History and Meaning of the Term Phoneme," supplement to *Le Maître Phonétique*, July–December, 1957, p. 3.

[21] Trubetzkoy, "La phonologie actuelle," *loc. cit.*, 230.

[22] Jones, "The History of the Term Phoneme," *loc. cit.*, 4.

[23] J. R. Firth, *Papers in Linguistics, 1934–1951*, 1.

[24] *Course in General Linguistics*, 82.

[25] Rulon Wells, "De Saussure's System of Linguistics," reprinted in Martin Joos (ed.), *Readings in Linguistics: The Development of Descriptive Linguistics in America Since 1925*, 4.

[26] W. F. Mackey, *Language Teaching Analysis*, 6.

[27] Gleason, *op. cit.*, 40.

[28] John T. Waterman, *Perspectives in Linguistics*, 69.

[29] Pierre Léon, *Laboratoire de langues et correction phonétique*, 46.

[30] Trubetzkoy, "La phonologie actuelle," *loc. cit.*, 231.

[31] Gleason, *op. cit.*, 43.

[32] Firth, *op. cit.*, 163.

[33] *Ibid.*

[34] Jesse Fewkes, "Anthropology," in George Brown Goode (ed.), *The Smithsonian Institution, 1846–1896*, 757.

[35] Gleason, *op. cit.*, 41.

[36] *Race, Language and Culture*, 206.

[37] Boas, *Handbook of American Indian Languages, Part I. Introduction*, 37.

[38] *Ibid.*, 26.

[39] *Ibid.*, 43.

[40] *Ibid.*, 28.

[41] *Ibid.*, 27.

[42] Gleason, *op. cit.*, 42.

[43] Sapir, *Language: An Introduction to the Study of Speech*, 49.

[44] *Ibid.*, 53.

[45] *Ibid.*, 26–28.

[46] *Ibid.*

[47] Sapir, *op. cit.*, 59.

[48] Cf. Francis, *op. cit.*, 208–20; Robert A. Hall, *Introductory Linguistics*, 138–45; Archibald A. Hill, *Introduction to Linguistic Structures*, 129–34.

[49] Hill, "Linguistic Science Since Bloomfield," *Quarterly Journal of Speech*, XLI (October, 1955), p. 253.

[50] Bloomfield, "A Set of Postulates for the Study of Language," *Language*, February, 1926, pp. 152–64.

[51] Bloomfield, *The Study of Language*.

Notes

52 *Linguistics and Reading*, 62.

53 "Leonard Bloomfield," *Language*, XXV (1949), 92.

54 Bloomfield, *The Study of Language*, 295.

55 Bloomfield, *Language*, 205.

56 Bloomfield, *Outline Guide for the Practical Study of Foreign Languages*, 8.

57 Bloomfield, *The Study of Language*, 302.

58 *Ibid.*

59 Ruth Hirsch, *Audio-Visual Aids in Language Teaching*, Monograph Series in Languages and Linguistics, No. 5 (March, 1954), 8.

60 "About Foreign Language Teaching," *Yale Review*, XXXIV, No. 4 (Summer, 1945), 628.

61 Catford, "The Teaching of English as a Foreign Language," in Randolph Quirk (ed.), *The Teaching of English*, 158.

62 Lado, *op. cit.*, 4.

63 Hall, "American Linguistics, 1925–1950," *Archivum Linguisticum*, IV (1952), 10.

64 Gouin, *The Art of Teaching and Studying Languages*.

65 *Ibid.*, 123.

66 *Ibid.*, 128.

67 *Ibid.*, 49.

68 *Ibid.*, 50.

69 *Ibid.*, 220.

70 *Ibid.*, 68.

71 *Ibid.*

72 *Ibid.*, 294.

73 Goldberger, *The Teaching of English to the Foreign-Born*, 41.

74 *Ibid.*, 42.

75 Frank V. Thompson, *Schooling of the Immigrant*, 174.

76 *Ibid.*, 190.

77 Both this and the following table are from Thompson's *Schooling of the Immigrant*, 170.

78 Sweet, *The Practical Study of Languages*, 75.

79 *Ibid.*, 177.

80 *Ibid.*, 100.

81 *Ibid.*, 38.

82 Sweet, *A Primer of Spoken English*, v.

83 *Ibid.*, x.

84 Sweet, *The Practical Study of Languages*, 93.

85 *Ibid.*, 70.

[86] *Ibid.*, 73.
[87] *Ibid.*, iv.
[88] *How to Teach a Foreign Language*, 11.
[89] *Ibid.*, 65.
[90] *Ibid.*
[91] *Ibid.*, 118.
[92] *Ibid.*, 172.
[93] Sweet, *The Practical Study of Languages.*
[94] Palmer, *The Principles of Language Study*, v.
[95] *The Oral Method of Teaching Languages*, 12.
[96] *Ibid.*, 15.
[97] *Ibid.*, 6.
[98] Palmer, *The Principles of Language Study*, 8.
[99] *Ibid.*, 13.
[100] *Ibid.*, 57.
[101] *Ibid.*, 132.
[102] *Ibid.*, 116.
[103] *Ibid.*, 117.
[104] Palmer, *The Oral Method of Teaching Languages*, 40.
[105] *A Grammar of Spoken English*, xxxii.
[106] *Ibid.*, xxxvii.
[107] Palmer, *The Scientific Study and Teaching of Languages*, 41.
[108] *Ibid.*, 39.

IV. The Growth of English as a Foreign Language, 1880–1940

[1] Marcus Lee Hansen, *The Immigrant in American History*, 21.
[2] *Ibid.*, 141.
[3] Edward Cieslak, *The Foreign Student in American Colleges*, 6.
[4] Reginald Wheeler, Henry King, and Alexander Davidson, *The Foreign Student in America*, 13.
[5] Samuel Capen, *Opportunities for Foreign Students at Colleges and Universities in the United States*, 52. For the number of foreign students, by years, see Appendix 3.
[6] Cieslak, *op. cit.*, 10.
[7] I. L. Kandel, *U. S. Activities in International Cultural Relations*, 39.
[8] Wheeler, King, and Davidson, *op. cit.*, 155.
[9] William E. Norris, "ELI: A Casual Chronology" (mimeographed), 1.
[10] Superintendent of Public Schools, Boston.

Notes

[11] Thompson, *op. cit.*, 21.

[12] Hansen, *op. cit.*, 17.

[13] Maurice Davie, *Refugees in America*, 107.

[14] *Ibid.*, 89.

[15] *Ibid.*

[16] *Ibid.*, 45–46.

[17] Robert Divine, *American Immigration Policy*, 1924–1952, 141.

V. Modern Foreign-Language Programs in the Early 1940's

[1] Paul F. Angiolillo, *Armed Forces Foreign Language Teaching—A Critical Evaluation and Implications*, 21.

[2] J. Milton Cowan and Mortimer Graves, "A Statement of Intensive Language Instruction," *German Quarterly*, Vol. XVII, No. 4, Part I (November, 1944), 165–67.

[3] Mortimer Graves and J. Milton Cowan, *Report of the First Year's Operation of the Intensive Language Program of the American Council of Learned Societies*, 4–5.

[4] Angiolillo, *op. cit.*, 29.

[5] *Ibid.*, 44.

[6] Berthold C. Friedl, "Techniques in Spoken Language: Specific Procedures in the Army Specialized Training Program Foreign Area and Language Studies," *Modern Language Journal*, Vol. XXVIII, No. 6 (October, 1944), 477.

[7] Méras, *op. cit.*, 51–53.

[8] *Ibid.*, 91.

[9] *Ibid.*, 106.

[10] Friedl, "Techniques in Spoken Languages," *loc. cit.*, 487.

[11] Hall, "Progress and Reaction in Modern Language Teaching," *Bulletin of the American Association of University Professors*, Vol. XXXI, No. 2 (Summer, 1945), 227.

[12] Helmut Rehder and W. Freeman Twaddell, "A.S.T.P. at Wisconsin," *German Quarterly*, Vol. XVII, No. 4, Part I (November, 1944), 216–23.

[13] Agard and Dunkel, *op. cit.*, 15.

[14] Hyneman, "The Wartime Area and Language Courses," *Bulletin of the American Association of University Professors*, Vol. XXXI, No. 3 (Autumn, 1945), 441.

[15] Most of the historical information on the ELI is from William E. Norris, "ELI: A Casual Chronology" (mimeographed).

[16] By 1962 enrollment had reached 130 annually, with total enrollment from 1942–65 over 1,000. *Ibid.*, 5.

[17] *Ibid.*, 6.

[18] Léon, *op. cit.*, 72.

[19] Fries, *Teaching and Learning English as a Foreign Language*, 3.

[20] *Ibid.*, 6.

[21] *Ibid.*, 32.

[22] *Ibid.*, 38.

[23] *Ibid.*, 7.

[24] Croft, "TESL Materials Development," in Kenneth Croft (ed.), *Selected Conference Papers of the Association of Teachers of English as a Second Language*, 42.

[25] Léon, *op. cit.*, 46.

[26] Croft, *op. cit.*, 46.

[27] *Ibid.*, 48.

[28] *Op. cit.*, 80.

[29] *American English Grammar*, 109.

[30] Fries, *The Structure of English*, 56.

[31] Gleason, *op. cit.*, 80.

[32] *Ibid.*, 1.

[33] Margaret Emmons, *Orientation and English Instruction for Students from Other Lands*, 17.

[34] Delattre, "Vers la méthode phonétique integral pour débutants," *French Review*, Vol. XVIII, No. 2 (December, 1944), 113.

[35] *Ibid.*

[36] *Ibid.*, 113.

[37] Delattre, "A Technique of Aural-Oral Approach," *French Review*, Vol. XX, No. 4 (February, 1947), 313.

[38] *Ibid.*, 320.

[39] Delattre, "Vers la méthode phonétique integral pour débutants," *loc. cit.*, 113.

[40] Agard and Dunkel, *op. cit.*, 248.

[41] *Ibid.*

[42] *Ibid.*, 3.

[43] Capen, *op. cit.*, 13.

[44] Institute of International Education, *Annual Report* (1933), 64.

[45] Institute of International Education, *Annual Report* (1949), 51.

[46] *The New York Times*, January 30, 1966.

[47] Institute of International Education, *Open Doors 1965*, 2. For a more detailed presentation of yearly growth in foreign student enrollment, see Appendix 3.

Notes

[48] DuBois, *Foreign Students and Higher Education in the United States*, 4.

[49] Sasnett, *op. cit.*, 3.

[50] Josef Mestenhauser, *Research in Programs for Foreign Students*, 21.

[51] Charles T. Scott, "Literature and the ESL Program," *Modern Language Journal*, Vol. XLVIII, No. 8 (December, 1964), 491.

[52] Committee on the Foreign Student in American Colleges and Universities, *The College, the University, and the Foreign Student*, 1.

[53] *Ibid.*

[54] Cieslak, *op. cit.*, 145.

[55] *Ibid.*, 149.

[56] DuBois, *op. cit.*, 209.

[57] Committee on Educational Interchange Policy, *A Foreign Student Program for the Developing Countries During the Coming Decades*, 2.

[58] National Association of Foreign Student Affairs, *Guidelines—English Language Proficiency*, 2.

[59] Committee on Educational Interchange Policy, *op. cit.*, 9.

[60] Committee on the Foreign Student in American Colleges and Universities, *op. cit.*, 14.

[61] DuBois, *op. cit.*, 209.

[62] Committee on Educational Interchange Policy, *The Goals of Student Exchange*, 5.

[63] Mestenhauser, *op. cit.*, 47.

[64] DuBois, *op. cit.*, 81.

[65] *Ibid.*, 83.

[66] Richard T. Morris, *The Two-Way Mirror: National Status in Foreign Student Adjustment*, 113.

VI. Principles and Methods: Linguistic Theory and Language Teaching

[1] Brooks, *Language and Language Learning*, 125.

[2] Fries, *Teaching and Learning English as a Foreign Language*, 3.

[3] Finocchiaro, *English as a Second Language: From Theory to Practice*, 39–46.

[4] Mackey, *op. cit.*, 165.

[5] Carroll, "A Primer of Programmed Instruction in Foreign Language Teaching," *International Review of Applied Linguistics in Language Teaching*, I, No. 2 (1963), 116.

[6] "English as a Second Language: Teaching," in Harold B. Allen (ed.), *Teaching English as a Second Language: A Book of Readings*, 88.

[7] Marty, *Language Laboratory Learning*, 24.

[8] "A Report on Programming a Basic Foreign Language Course," in David P. Harris (ed.), *Selected Conference Papers of the National Association of Foreign Student Affairs English Language Section, 1962. NAFSA Studies and Papers, English Language Series No. 8*, 9–13.

[9] *Ibid.*

[10] Hill, "Linguistic Science Since Bloomfield," *loc. cit.*, 253.

[11] Agard and Dunkel, *op. cit.*, 287.

[12] Léon, "Teaching Pronunciation," in Albert Valdman (ed.), *Trends in Language Teaching*, 74.

[13] *Ibid.*, 76.

[14] Marty, *op. cit.*, 22.

[15] "Some Techniques for Bridging the Gap," in Robert P. Fox (ed.), *The 1964 Conference Papers of the Association of Teachers of English as a Second Language of the National Association of Foreign Student Affairs*, 51.

[16] Lado, *Language Teaching*, 125.

[17] Politzer, *Foreign Language Learning. A Linguistic Introduction. Preliminary Edition*, 72.

[18] Mackey, *op. cit.*, 199.

[19] W. F. Twadell, "Linguistics and Language Teachers," in Carol Kreidler (ed.), *On Teaching English to Speakers of Other Languages*, 76.

[20] *Ibid.*, 77.

[21] *Ibid.*

[22] Agard and Dunkel, *op. cit.*, 273.

[23] Bloomfield, *Language*, 277.

[24] Agard and Dunkel, *op. cit.*, 275.

[25] Mackey, *op. cit.*, 218.

[26] West, *A General Service List of English Words*, 184.

[27] Méras, *op. cit.*, 25.

[28] Agard and Dunkel, *op. cit.*, 35.

[29] Lado, *op. cit.*, 93.

[30] *Ibid.*

[31] *Linguistics and Reading*, 26.

[32] *Op. cit.*, 15.

[33] *Trends in Linguistics*, 203.

[34] Benjamin Elson and Velma Pickett, *An Introduction to Morphology and Syntax*, 57.

[35] *Ibid.*, 75.

Notes

[36] William Moulton, "Applied Linguistics in the Classroom," in Harold B. Allen (ed.), *Teaching English as a Second Language*, 81. For descriptions of a wide range of pattern practice exercises, see Lado, *op. cit.*, 106–10; Brooks, *op. cit.*, 156–63; also Moulton, *A Linguistic Guide to Language Learning*, 75–76.

[37] Francis, *op. cit.*, 293.

[38] Hockett, *A Course in Modern Linguistics*, 152.

[39] R. H. Robins, *General Linguistics: An Introductory Survey*, 232.

[40] Politzer, *op. cit.*, 5.

[41] Francis W. Gravit and Albert Valdman, "Structural Drills in the Language Laboratory," *International Journal of American Linguistics*, XXIX, No. 2 (April, 1963), 13.

[42] Richard Gunter, "A Problem in Transformational Teaching," in Harold B. Allen (ed.), *Teaching English as a Second Language*, 201.

[43] Hill, "The Promises and Limitations of the Newest Type of Grammatical Analysis," *TESOL Quarterly*, I, No. 2 (June, 1967), 13.

[44] Politzer, *op. cit.*, 15.

[45] Newmark, "Grammatical Theory and the Teaching of English as a Foreign Language," in Harris (ed.), *The 1963 Conference Papers of the English Language Section of the National Association of Foreign Student Affairs*, 6.

[46] *Ibid.*, 7.

[47] Valdman (ed.), *op. cit.*, xix.

[48] *Ibid.*

[49] Saporta, "Applied Linguistics and Generative Grammar," *ibid.*, 82.

[50] *Ibid.*, 84.

[51] *Ibid.*, 86.

[52] Newmark, "Grammatical Theory and the Teaching of English as a Foreign Language," in Harris (ed.), *The 1963 Conference Papers*, 5.

[53] Marty, *op. cit.*, 25.

[54] Prator, "English as a Second Language," in Harold B. Allen (ed.), *Teaching English as a Second Language*, 91.

[55] Prator, "Development of a Manipulation-Communication Scale," in Robert P. Fox (ed.), *The 1964 Conference Papers of the Association of Teachers of English as a Second Language of the National Association for Foreign Student Affairs*, 60.

[56] *Ibid.*, 61.

[57] Lado, *op. cit.*, 113.

[58] Ilson, "The Dicto-Comp: A Specialized Technique for Controlling Speech and Writing in Language Learning," *Language Learning*, X, No. 4 (1962), 299.

[59] "Pattern Practice for Reading," *Language Learning*, XIV, Nos. 3–4 (1964), 133.

[60] *Ibid.*, 127–35.

[61] Howard Nostrand, "Describing and Teaching the Sociocultural Context of a Foreign Language and Literature," in Valdman (ed.), *op. cit.*, 4–5.

[62] Virginia Allen, "Preparation of Dialogue and Narrative Material for Students of English as a Foreign Language," in Harold B. Allen (ed.), *Teaching English as a Second Language*, 184.

[63] Léon, *op. cit.*, 25.

[64] Jespersen, *op. cit.*, 178.

[65] Léon, *op. cit.*, 36–39.

[66] Valdman (ed.), *op. cit.*, xv.

[67] Joseph C. Hutchinson, *The Language Laboratory . . . How Effective Is It?* 4–9.

[68] Luis James Valverde, "Multi-Disciplinary Bases for the Teaching-Learning of English as a Second Language" (unpublished Ph.D. dissertation, University of California at Los Angeles, 1960), 82–88.

[69] See Léon, *op. cit.*; Marty, *op. cit.*; Don R. Iodice, *Guidelines to Language Teaching in Classroom and Laboratory*; Edward Stack, *The Language Laboratory and Modern Language Teaching*.

[70] Valdman (ed.), *op. cit.*, xxii.

VII. EFL Teaching Overseas

[1] William Riley Parker, *The National Interest and Foreign Languages*, 3.

[2] Catford, "The Progress of Teaching English as a Second Language Overseas," in Croft (ed.), *op. cit.*, 32.

[3] Parker, *op. cit.*, 97–98.

[4] Denis Giraud, "New Trends in Language Teaching in France," in Harris, (ed.), *The 1963 Conference Papers*, 20.

[5] Ruth Sutherlin, "The Language Situation in East Africa," in Frank Rice (ed.), *Study of the Role of Second Languages in Asia, Africa and Latin America*, 65.

[6] English Program, *Outline Report on the Position and Teaching of English in India*, 3.

[7] Gordon K. Fairbanks and Bal Govind Misra, *Spoken and Written Hindi*, v.

[8] English Program, *Outline Report on the Position and Teaching of English in India*, 3.

[9] *Ibid.*, 2.

Notes

[10] Punya Sloka Ray, "Language Standardization," in Rice (ed.), *op. cit.*, 96.

[11] Center for Applied Linguistics, *English Overseas*, 1.

[12] Janet Roberts, "Sociocultural Change and Communication Problems," in Rice (ed.), *op. cit.*, 108.

[13] *Ibid.*, 106. Based on UNESCO figures.

[14] Center for Applied Linguistics, *English Overseas*, 5.

[15] Center for Applied Linguistics, *University Resources in the United States for Linguistics and the Teaching of English as a Foreign Language*, 44–45.

[16] Sirapi Ohannessian and Lois McArdle, *A Survey of Twelve University Programs for the Preparation of Teachers of English to Speakers of Other Languages*.

[17] Center for Applied Linguistics, *English Overseas*, 13.

[18] *Ibid.*, 12.

[19] Charles Ferguson, "The Language Factor in National Development," in Rice (ed.), *op. cit.*, 12.

[20] Catford, "The Progress of Teaching English as a Second Language Overseas," in Croft (ed.), *op. cit.*, 33.

[21] Center for Applied Linguistics, *English Overseas*, 23.

[22] *Ibid.*, 14.

[23] Parker, *op. cit.*, 7.

[24] Center for Applied Linguistics, *English Overseas*, 3.

[25] Parker, *op. cit.*, 77.

[26] Albert Marckwardt, "Opportunities and Obligations," *Language*, XL, No. 3, Part 2 (July–September, 1964), 33.

[27] Trusten Russell, "Opportunities for Service Offered by Government Agencies," in Kreidler (ed.), *op. cit.*, 14.

[28] *Ibid.*, 15.

[29] *Ibid.*, 16.

[30] Prator, "Teaching English Overseas," in Kreidler (ed.), *op. cit.*, 4.

[31] George E. Perren, "British Teaching of English in the Commonwealth," in Harris (ed.), *The 1963 Conference Papers*, 15.

[32] Valdman (ed.), *op. cit.*, xx.

[33] Uriel Weinreich, *Languages in Contact*, 3.

[34] Lado, *Linguistics Across Cultures*, 11.

[35] *Ibid.*, 27.

[36] Earl Stevick, Marianne Lehr, and Paul Imhoff (eds.), *An Active Introduction to Swahili: Geography*, 126.

[37] T. Kandiah, "The Teaching of English in Ceylon: Some Problems in

Contrastive Statement," *Language Learning*, XV, Nos. 3–4 (1965), 150.

[38] Carroll, "Linguistic Relativity, Contrastive Analysis, and Language Learning," *International Review of Applied Linguistics in Language Teaching*, I, No. 1 (1963), 17.

[39] Politzer, *Foreign Language Learning*, 73.

[40] Fairbanks and Misra, *op. cit.*, 76, 114, and 130.

VIII. *Conclusion*

[1] Catford, "Teaching English as a Foreign Language," in Quirk (ed.), *op. cit.*, 139.

[2] *Op. cit.*, 79.

APPENDIX I. *Development of EFL Courses, 1880–1940*

[1] Frederic E. Farrington, *Public Facilities for Educating the Alien*, 27.

[2] *Ibid.*

[3] American Civic League, *Education of the Immigrant*, 34.

[4] University of the State of New York, *Organization of Schools in English for the Foreign-Born*.

[5] Edith Abbott, *Immigration: Selected Documents and Case Records*, 572.

[6] Farrington, *op. cit.*, 36–51.

[7] Walter F. Wilcox, *Studies in American Demography*, 455.

[8] American Civic League, *op. cit.*, 48.

[9] *Ibid.*, 40.

[10] Frank V. Thompson, *Schooling of the Immigrant*, 50.

[11] Edith Abbott, *op. cit.*, 566.

[12] Massachusetts, Board of Education, *A Teacher's Handbook to Accompany Standard Lessons in English for American Citizenship*, Department of University Extension bulletin, IV, No. 3 (May, 1919), 7.

[13] Edith Abbott, *op. cit.*, 567.

[14] Connecticut, State Board of Education, *A Statement Concerning the Provisions of the Laws Governing Schools and Classes for Non-English-Speaking Adults*, 3.

[15] Connecticut, State Board of Education, *Classes for Foreign-Born Adults*, 10.

[16] *Ibid.*, 14.

[17] *Ibid.*, 16.

[18] S. J. Brown, *A Suggested Course of Study and Syllabus for Non-English-Speaking Adults*.

[19] Lester K. Ade, *Pennsylvania Program for Literacy and Citizenship Education*, 12.

[20] Donald M. Cresswell (ed.), *Illiteracy, Non-English Speaking and Alien Problems and their Solutions*, 33.

[21] Ade, *op. cit.*, 10.

[22] Cresswell, *op. cit.*, 44.

[23] Farrington, *op. cit.*, 15.

[24] Wilcox, *op. cit.*

[25] Thompson, *op. cit.*, 54.

[26] Philip Davis, *Immigration and Americanization*, 575.

[27] Thompson, *op. cit.*, 60.

[28] Ethel Richardson, *Immigrant Education Manual*, 10.

[29] *Ibid.*, 11.

[30] *Ibid.*

[31] *Ibid.*, 12.

[32] *Ibid.*, 13.

[33] California, Department of Education, Division of Immigrant Education, *Lessons in Oral English for Beginners in Rural Schools*, Bulletin No. 5–E (1924), 9.

[34] *Ibid.*, 3.

[35] California, Department of Education, *California History: Lessons in English for Intermediate and Advanced Classes of Adults*, Bulletin No. 1 (1934).

[36] *Ibid.*, 13.

APPENDIX 2. *Analysis of Early EFL Texts*

[1] Chancellor, *Reading and Language Lessons for Evening Schools*, iii.

[2] *Ibid.*

[3] *Ibid.*, 87.

[4] *Ibid.*, 25–32.

[5] *Ibid.*, 83.

[6] Sarah O'Brien, *English for Foreigners, Book One*, iv.

[7] *Ibid.*, iv–v.

[8] *Ibid.*, v.

[9] O'Brien, *English for Foreigners, Book Two*, v.

[10] *Ibid.*, 20.

[11] Prior and Ryan, *How to Learn English*, 2–3.

[12] *Ibid.*, vii.

[13] *Ibid.*, v.

[14] Houghton, *First Lessons in English for Foreigners in Evening Schools,* 6.

[15] *Ibid.,* 84.

[16] Houghton, *Second Book in English for Foreigners in Evening Schools.*

[17] Austin, *Lessons in English for Foreign Women,* 12.

[18] *Ibid.,* 13.

[19] *Ibid.,* 21.

[20] Beshgeturian, *Foreigners' Guide to English,* 30.

[21] *Ibid.,* 161.

[22] Page v.

[23] Page xiii.

[24] Page xv.

[25] Page xvi.

[26] Page 8.

[27] Page 9.

[28] Page 21.

APPENDIX 5. *Trends in EFL Teaching in the 1950's and 1960's*

[1] Harris, *A Survey of Intermediate-Level Programs of College English for Foreign Students.*

[2] Harris, *A Survey of English Language Requirements and Facilities for Foreign Students in United States Institutions of Higher Learning, 1961.*

[3] Institute of International Education, *English Language and Orientation Programs in the United States.*

[4] English Program, *Academic Year Programs in English for Foreign Students.*

[5] Harold B. Allen, *A Survey of the Teaching of English to Non-English Speakers in the United States.*

[6] "Survey of Programs in English as a Second Language at the Intermediate and Advanced Levels, Prepared for the Association of Teachers of English as a Second Language, NAFSA" (Survey Committee, University of Illinois, 1967). A summary also appeared in the *NAFSA Newsletter,* Vol. X, No. 5 (February, 1967), 6–7.

[7] The figures in parentheses refer to the large school in contrast with the small school offering.

Bibliography

Abbott, Edith. *Immigration: Select Documents and Case Records.* Chicago, University of Chicago Press, 1924.

Abbott, Grace. *The Immigrant and the Community.* New York, The Century Company, 1917.

Ade, Lester K. *Pennsylvania Program for Literacy and Citizenship Education. Bulletin No. 293,* Harrisburg, Pennsylvania, Department of Public Instruction. Harrisburg, 1938.

Agard, Frederick B., and Harold B. Dunkel. *An Investigation of Second Language Teaching.* Boston, Ginn and Company, 1948.

Albright, Robert W. "The I.P.A.: Its Backgrounds and Development," *International Journal of American Linguistics,* Vol. XXIV, No. 1, Part 3 (1958).

Allen, Harold B., ed. *Readings in Applied English Linguistics.* 2d ed. New York, Appleton-Century-Crofts, 1964.

——. *A Survey of the Teaching of English to Non-English Speakers in the United States.* Champaign, Illinois, National Council of Teachers of English, 1966.

——, ed. *Teaching English as a Second Language: A Book of Readings.* New York, McGraw-Hill Book Company, 1965.

Allen, Virginia French, ed. *On Teaching English to Speakers of Other Languages.* Champaign, Illinois, National Council of Teachers of English, 1965.

American Civic League. *Education of the Immigrant. Bulletin No. 51,* U.S. Bureau of Education. Washington, 1913.

Angiolillo, Paul F. *Armed Forces Foreign Language Teaching: A Critical Evaluation and Implications.* New York, S. F. Vanni, 1947.

Axelrod, Joseph. "The Navy Language School Program and Foreign Languages in Schools and Colleges: Aims and Techniques," *Modern Language Journal,* Vol. XXIX (January, 1945), 40–47.

Bach, Emmon. *An Introduction to Transformational Grammars.* New York, Holt, Rinehart and Winston, 1964.

Bagster-Collins, E. W. *The History of Modern Language Teaching in the United States.* New York, Macmillan, 1930.

Baugh, Albert C. *A History of the English Language.* New York, Appleton-Century-Crofts, 1957.

Bell, Alexander Melville. *Visible Speech.* London, Simpkin, Marshall and Company, 1867.

Bloch, Bernard, and George L. Trager. *An Outline of Linguistic Analysis.* Baltimore, Linguistic Society of America, 1942.

Bloomfield, Leonard. "About Foreign Language Teaching," *Yale Review,* Vol. XXXIV, No. 4 (Summer, 1945), 624–41.

———. *Language.* New York, Henry Holt, 1933.

———. "On Recent Works in General Linguistics," *Modern Philology,* Vol. XXV (1927), 211–30.

———. *Outline Guide for the Practical Study of Foreign Languages.* Baltimore, Linguistic Society of America, 1942.

———. "A Set of Postulates for the Study of Language," *Language* (February, 1926), 153–64.

———. *The Study of Language.* New York, Henry Holt, 1914.

Boas, Franz. *Handbook of American Indian Languages. Part I, Introduction.* Washington, Government Printing Office, 1911.

———. *Race, Language, and Culture.* New York, Macmillan, 1940.

Braun, W. A. "The University in Americanization," *Columbia University Quarterly,* Vol. XXI, No. 3 (July, 1919), 244–47.

Bridgeport Public Library. *Aids to Foreigners Learning English.* Bridgeport, Connecticut, Bridgeport Public Library, 1916.

Brooks, Nelson. *Language and Language Learning.* 2d ed. New York, Harcourt, Brace and World, 1964.

Brown, S. J. *A Suggested Course of Study and Syllabus for Non-English-Speaking Adults.* Hartford, Connecticut, State Board of Education, 1918.

Butler, Fred. *State Americanization. Bulletin No. 77*, U.S. Bureau of Education. Washington, 1919.

Cadet, Felix. *Port-Royal Education: A Sketch of Its History with Extracts from Its Leading Authors*. Syracuse, New York, C. W. Bardeen, 1899.

California, Department of Education. *California History: Lessons in English for Intermediate and Advanced Classes of Adults. Bulletin No. 1*. Sacramento, California State Printing Office, 1934.

———, Department of Education. Division of Immigrant Education. *Lessons in Oral English for Beginners in Rural Schools*. Bulletin 5–E. Sacramento, California State Printing Office, 1924.

———. *Lessons in Oral English for Classes of Beginners—Women*. Bulletin 5–D. Sacramento, California State Printing Office, 1924.

Capen, Samuel. *Opportunities for Foreign Students at Colleges and Universities in the United States. Bulletin No. 27*, U.S. Bureau of Education. Washington, 1915.

Carroll, John B. "Linguistic Relativity, Contrastive Analysis, and Language Learning," *International Review of Applied Linguistics In Language Teaching*, Vol. I, No. 1 (1963), 1–20.

———. "A Primer of Programmed Instruction in Foreign Language Teaching," *International Review of Applied Linguistics in Language Teaching*, Vol. I, No. 2 (1963), 115–42.

———. *The Study of Language*, Cambridge, Harvard University Press, 1961.

Center for Applied Linguistics. *English Overseas*. Washington, Center for Applied Linguistics, 1961.

———. *University Resources in the United States for Linguistics and the Teaching of English as a Foreign Language*. Washington, Center for Applied Linguistics, 1963.

Cieslak, Edward. *The Foreign Student in American Colleges*. Detroit, Wayne University Press, 1955.

Cochran, Anne. *Modern Methods of Teaching English as a Foreign Language*. Washington, Educational Services, 1952.

Cole, Robert, and James Thorp. *Modern Foreign Languages and Their Teaching*. New York, Appleton-Century Company, 1937.

Coleman, Algernon. *The Teaching of Modern Foreign Languages in the United States*. New York, Macmillan Company, 1929.

Columbia University Extension Teaching Announcement. New York, Columbia University, 1911, 1915, 1920, 1925.

Comenius, John Amos. *The Analytic Didactic of Comenius.* Translated, with an introduction, by Vladimir Jelinek. Chicago, University of Chicago Press, 1953.

Committee on Educational Interchange Policy. *The Foreign Student: Exchangee or Immigrant.* New York, Institute of International Education, 1958.

———. *A Foreign Student Program for the Developing Countries During the Coming Decades.* New York, Institute of International Education, 1962.

———. *The Goals of Student Exchange.* New York, Institute of International Education, 1955.

Committee on the Foreign Student in American Colleges and Universities. *The College, the University and the Foreign Student.* New York, NAFSA, 1963.

Connecticut, State Board of Education. *Classes for Foreign-Born Adults.* Hartford, State Board of Education, 1920.

———. *A Statement Concerning the Provisions of the Laws Governing Schools and Classes for Non-English-Speaking Adults.* Hartford, State Board of Education, 1921.

Cowan, J. Milton, and Mortimer Graves. "A Statement of Intensive Language Instruction," *German Quarterly,* Vol. XVII, No. 4, Part I (November, 1944), 165–67.

Cresswell, Donald M., ed. *Illiteracy, Non-English Speaking and Alien Problems and their Solutions. Bulletin No. 104,* Harrisburg, Pennsylvania Department of Public Instruction. Harrisburg, 1935.

Croft, Kenneth, ed. *Selected Conference Papers of the Association of Teachers of English as a Second Language.* New York, NAFSA, 1965.

Danielsson, Bror. *John Hart's Works on English Orthography and Pronunciation.* Stockholm, Almqvist and Wiksell, 1955.

Darian, Steven. "Backgrounds of Modern Language Teaching: Sweet, Jespersen, and Palmer," *Modern Language Journal,* Vol. LIII, No. 8 (December, 1969), 545–50.

———. "Trends in EFL Teaching at American Universities," *TESOL Quarterly* (September, 1969), 221–29.

Bibliography

Davie, Maurice R. *Refugees in America*. New York, Harper and Brothers, 1947.

Davis, Philip. *Immigration and Americanization*. Boston, Ginn and Company, 1920.

DeCamp, David. "The Training of English Teachers in the Far East," *Language Learning*, Vol. XV, Nos. 3–4 (1965), 119–27.

Delattre, Pierre. "Vers la méthode phonétique integral pour débutants," *French Review*, Vol. XVIII, No. 2 (December, 1944), 108–15.

———. "A Technique of Aural-Oral Approach," *French Review*, Vol. XX, No. 3 (January, 1947), 238–51; Vol. XX, No. 4 (February, 1947), 311–24.

Department of Commerce and Labor. *13th Census of the United States, 1910. Abstract of the Census*. Washington, Government Printing Office, 1913.

Department of Interior, Census Office. *Compendium of the 11th Census, 1890*. Washington, Government Printing Office, 1892.

———. *Compendium of the Tenth Census (June 1, 1880)*. Washington, Government Printing Office, 1883.

Divine, Robert. *American Immigration Policy, 1924–1952*. New Haven, Yale University Press, 1957.

DuBois, Cora. *Foreign Students and Higher Education in the United States*. Washington, American Council on Education, 1956.

Elson, Benjamin, and Velma Pickett. *An Introduction to Morphology and Syntax*. Santa Ana, California, Summer Institute of Linguistics, 1964.

Emmons, Margaret L. *Orientation and English Instruction for Students from Other Lands*. Washington, Federal Security Agency–Office of Education, 1950.

English Program. *Academic Year Programs in English for Foreign Students*. Washington, Center for Applied Linguistics, 1967.

———. *Outline Report on the Position and Teaching of English in India*. Washington, Center for Applied Linguistics, 1966.

Fairbanks, Gordon K., and Bal Govind Misra. *Spoken and Written Hindi*. Ithaca, New York, Cornell University Press, 1966.

Farrington, Frederic E. *Public Facilities for Educating the Alien. Bulletin No. 18*, U.S. Bureau of Education. Washington, 1916.

Finocchiaro, Mary. *English as a Second Language: From Theory to Practice.* New York, Regents Publishing Company, 1965.

Firth, J. R. *Papers in Linguistics, 1934–1951.* London, Oxford, 1957.

Fishman, Joshua, et al. *Language Loyalties in the U.S.: the Maintenance and Perpetuation of Non-English Mother Tongues by American Ethnic and Religious Groups.* Washington, U.S. Office of Education, 1964.

Fox, Edith, Curator and University Archivist. Letter to Author, Cornell University, October 6, 1966.

Fox, Robert P., ed. *The 1964 Conference Papers of the Association of Teachers of English as a Second Language of the National Association for Foreign Student Affairs.* New York, NAFSA, 1965.

Francis, W. Nelson. *The Structure of English.* New York, Ronald Press, 1956.

Frank, Marcella. *Annotated Bibliography of Materials for English as a Second Language.* New York, NAFSA, 1960.

Friedl, Berthold C. "Techniques in Spoken Languages: Specific Procedures in the ASTP Foreign Area and Language Studies," *Modern Language Journal*, Vol. XXVIII, No. 6 (October, 1944), 476–98.

Fries, Charles C. *American English Grammar.* New York, Appleton-Century-Crofts, 1940.

———. "American Linguistics and the Teaching of English," *Language Learning*, Nos. 1–2 (1955), 1–22.

———. *Linguistics and Reading.* New York, Holt, Rinehart, and Winston, 1962.

———. *The Structure of English.* New York, Harcourt, Brace and Company, 1952.

———. *Teaching and Learning English as a Foreign Language.* Ann Arbor, University of Michigan Press, 1945.

Fryer, John. *Admission of Chinese Students to American Colleges. Bulletin No. 2*, U.S. Bureau of Education. Washington, 1909.

Ganss, George E. *Saint Ignatius' Idea of a Jesuit University.* Milwaukee, Marquette University Press, 1954.

Gleason, H. A. *An Introduction to Descriptive Linguistics.* New York, Holt, Rinehart and Winston, 1961.

———. *Linguistics and English Grammar.* New York, Holt, Rinehart and Winston, 1965.

Bibliography

Goldberger, Henry H. *The Teaching of English to the Foreign-Born. Bulletin No. 80.* U.S. Bureau of Education. Washington, 1919.

Goode, George Brown, ed. *The Smithsonian Institution, 1846–1896.* Washington, The Smithsonian Institution, 1897.

Gouin, François. *The Art of Teaching and Studying Languages.* Translated by Howard Swan and Victor Betis. 9th ed. New York and London, Longmans, Green and Company, 1919.

Grammont, Maurice. *Traité de Phonétique.* Paris, Libraire Delagrave, 1933.

Grandgent, C. H., et al. *Methods of Teaching Modern Languages.* Boston, D. C. Heath and Company, 1904.

Graves, Mortimer, and J. M. Cowan. *Report of the First Year's Operation of the Intensive Language Program of the American Council of Learned Societies.* New York, American Council of Learned Societies, 1942.

Gravit, Francis W., and Albert Valdman. "Structural Drills in the Language Laboratory," *International Journal of American Linguistics,* Vol. XXIX, No. 2 (April, 1963).

Gray, Louis. *Foundations of Language.* New York, Macmillan Company, 1939.

Greene, Samuel. *First Lessons in Grammar Based on the Construction and Analysis of Sentences.* Philadelphia, Cowperthwait, Desilver and Butler, 1848.

———. *A Treatise on the Structure of the English Language.* Philadelphia, H. Cowperthwait and Sons, 1862.

Gumperz, John, and June Rumery. *Conversational Hindu-Urdu.* Berkeley, University of California Press, 1962.

Gwynn, Aubrey. *Roman Education from Cicero to Quintilian.* Oxford, Clarendon Press, 1926.

Hall, Robert A. "American Linguistics, 1925–1950," *Archivum Linguisticum,* Vol. III (March, 1951), 101–25, and Vol. IV (1952), 1–16.

———. *Introductory Linguistics.* Philadelphia, Chilton Books, 1964.

———. "Progress and Reaction in Modern Language Teaching," *Bulletin of American Association of University Professors,* Vol. XXXI, No. 2 (Summer, 1945), 220–30.

Halliday, N. A. K., Angus McIntosh, and Peter Stevens. *The Linguistic Sciences and Language Teaching.* London, Longmans, 1964.

Hammer, John H., and Frank A. Rice. *A Bibliography of Contrastive Linguistics*. Washington, Center for Applied Linguistics, 1965.

Hamp, Eric. *A Glossary of American Technical Linguistic Usage, 1925–1950*. Utrecht, Spectrum Publishers, 1957.

Handschin, Charles H. *The Teaching of Modern Languages in the United States. Bulletin No. 3*, U.S. Bureau of Education. Washington, 1913.

Hansen, Marcus Lee. *The Immigrant in American History*. Cambridge, Harvard, 1948.

Harris, David P. *A Survey of English Language Requirements and Facilities for Foreign Students in United States Institutions of Higher Learning, 1961*. New York, NAFSA, 1962.

———. *A Survey of Intermediate-Level Programs of College English for Foreign Students*. New York, NAFSA, 1956.

———, ed. *The 1963 Conference Papers of the English Language Section of the National Association of Foreign Student Affairs*. New York, NAFSA, 1964.

———, ed. *Selected Conference Papers of the NAFSA English Language Section, 1962. NAFSA Studies and Papers, English Language Series No. 8*. New York, NAFSA, 1964.

Hill, Archibald A. *Introduction to Linguistic Structures*. New York, Harcourt, Brace and Company, 1958.

———. "Language Analysis and Language Teaching," *Modern Language Journal*, Vol. XL (October, 1956), 335–45.

———. "Linguistic Science Since Bloomfield," *Quarterly Journal of Speech*, Vol. XLI (October, 1955), 235–60.

———. "The Promises and Limitations of the Newest Type of Grammatical Analysis," *TESOL Quarterly*, Vol. I, No. 2 (June, 1967), 10–22.

Hirsch, Ruth. *Audio-Visual Aids in Language Teaching*. Monograph Series of Languages and Linguistics, No. 6. Washington, Georgetown University Press, 1954.

Hockett, Charles. *A Course in Modern Linguistics*. New York, Macmillan Company, 1958.

Hoole, Charles. *A New Discovery of the Old Art of Teaching Schoole*. Facsimile, edited with an introduction by Thiselton Mark. London, Andrew Cook, 1660.

Bibliography

Hughes, John P. *The Science of Language.* New York, Random House, 1962.

Hutchinson, Joseph C. *The Language Laboratory . . . How Effective Is It?* Washington, U.S. Department of Health, Education, and Welfare, 1964.

Hyneman, Charles S. "The Wartime Area and Language Courses," *Bulletin of American Association of University Professors,* Vol. XXXI, No. 3 (Autumn, 1945), 434–48.

Ilson, Robert. "The Dicto-Comp: A Specialized Technique for Controlling Speech and Writing in Language Learning," *Language Learning,* Vol. X, No. 4 (1962).

Institute of International Education. *Annual Report of the Director.* New York, Institute of International Education, 1926, 1927, 1929–1931, 1933, 1935–1937, 1939, 1943, 1944, 1946, 1947, 1949.

―――. *Educational Exchange in the Atlantic Area.* New York, Institute of International Education, 1965.

―――. *Education for One World.* New York, Institute of International Education, 1950.

―――. *English Language and Orientation Programs in the United States.* New York, Institute of International Education, 1964.

―――. *Open Doors 1965.* New York, Institute of International Education, 1965.

Iodice, Don R. *Guidelines to Language Teaching in Classroom and Laboratory.* Washington, Electronic Teaching Laboratories, 1961.

Ivič, Milka. *Trends in Linguistics.* The Hague, Mouton and Company, 1965.

Jespersen, Otto. *How to Teach a Foreign Language.* London, George Allen and Unwin, 1904.

Jewett, J. L. *Ollendorf's New Method of Learning to Read, Write, and Speak the French Language.* New York, D. Appleton and Company, 1847.

Jones, Daniel. "The History and Meaning of the Term Phoneme," Supplement to *Le Maître Phonétique,* July–December, 1957, pp. 1–20.

Jones, Maldwyn. *American Immigration.* Chicago, University of Chicago Press, 1960.

Kandel, I. L. *U.S. Activities in International Cultural Relations.* Washington, American Council on Education, 1954.

English as a Foreign Language

Kandiah, T. "The Teaching of English in Ceylon: Some Problems in Contrastive Statement," *Language Learning*, Vol. XV, Nos. 3–4 (1965), 147–66.

Kirkham, Samuel. *English Grammar in Familiar Lectures*. New York, Robert B. Collins, 1829.

Kreidler, Carol J., ed. *On Teaching English to Speakers of Other Languages*. Series II. Champaign, Illinois, National Council of Teachers of English, 1966.

Lado, Robert. *Language Teaching*. New York, McGraw-Hill, 1964.
———. *Linguistics Across Cultures*. Ann Arbor, University of Michigan Press, 1957.

Lane, George S. "Changes of Emphasis in Linguistics with particular reference to Paul and Bloomfield," *Studies in Philology*, Vol. XLII (1945), 468–83.

Larude, Faze. "Language Teaching in Historical Perspective." Unpublished Ph.D. dissertation, University of Michigan, 1964.

Laurie, S. S. *John Amos Comenius*. Syracuse, New York, C. W. Bardeen, 1892.

Leavitt, Sturgis E. "The Teaching of Spanish in the United States," *Hispania*, Vol. XLIV, No. 4 (December, 1961), 591–625.

Léon, Pierre R. *Laboratoire de langues et correction phonétique*. Paris, Didier, 1962.

Leonard, Sterling. *Doctrines of Correctness in English Usage, 1700–1800*. Madison, University of Wisconsin, 1929.

Lyman, Rollo. *English Grammar in American Schools before 1850*. *Bulletin No. 12*, U.S. Office of Education. Washington, 1922.

Mackey, W. F. *Language Teaching Analysis*. London, Longmans Green, 1965.

McKenzie, T. R. "The Teaching of English to Non-English-Speaking Immigrants to Canada." Unpublished Ph.D. dissertation, University of Toronto, 1954.

Mahoney, John J., and Charles M. Herlihey. *First Steps in Americanization*. Boston, Houghton Mifflin, 1918.

Marcel, Claude. *The Study of Languages*. New York, Appleton and Company, 1885.

Marckwardt, Albert. "Opportunities and Obligations," *Language,* Vol. XL, No. 3, Part II (July–September, 1964), 26–37.

———. "TEFL," *Linguistic Reporter*, Vol. V, No. 4 (August, 1963).

Marrou, Henry I. *Histoire de l'Education dans l'Antiquité*. Paris, Éditions du Seuil, 1948.

Marty, Ferdinand. *Language Laboratory Learning*. Wellesley, Massachusetts, Audio-Visual Publications, 1960.

Massachusetts, Board of Education. *English for American Citizenship*. Department of University Extension bulletin, III, No. 4, July, 1918.

———. *A Teacher's Handbook to Accompany Standard Lessons in English for American Citizenship*. Department of University Extension bulletin, IV, No. 3, May, 1919.

Matthew, Robert J. *Language and Area Studies in the Armed Services*. Washington, American Council on Education, 1947.

Méras, Edmond A. *A Language Teacher's Guide*. New York, Harper and Brothers, 1954.

Mestenhauser, Josef. *Research in Programs for Foreign Students*. New York, NAFSA, 1961.

Mohrmann, Christine, Alf Sommerfelt, and J. Whatmough. *Trends in European and American Linguistics 1930–1960*. Utrecht, Spectrum Publishers, 1961.

Monroe, Will S. *Comenius and the Beginning of Educational Reform*. New York, Charles Scribner's Sons, 1900.

Morris, Richard T. *The Two-Way Mirror: National Status in Foreign Student Adjustment*. Minneapolis, University of Minnesota Press, 1960.

Moulton, William. *A Linguistic Guide to Language Learning*. New York, Modern Language Association, 1966.

Murray, Lindley. *English Grammar adapted to the different classes of learners*. 29th ed. Philadelphia, Brown and Peters, 1829.

National Association of Foreign Student Affairs. *Guidelines—English Language Proficiency*. New York, NAFSA, 1965.

National Association of Foreign Student Affairs and the Institute of International Education. *Research in International Education*. New York, NAFSA and Institute of International Education, 1966.

National Council of Teachers of English. *The National Interest and the Teaching of English as a Second Language*. Champaign, Illinois, 1961.

Norris, William E. "ELI: A Casual Chronology." Ann Arbor, English Language Institute, 1966. Mimeographed.

North American Civic League. *Annual Report, 1908–1909.* Boston, North American Civic League, 1909.

———. *Annual Report, 1909–1910.* Boston, North American Civic League, 1910.

Nostrand, Howard L., et al. *Research on Language Teaching: An Annotated Bibliography for 1945–1961.* Seattle, University of Washington Press, 1962.

Ohannessian, Sirapi. *Reference List of Materials for English as a Foreign Language.* Washington, Center for Applied Linguistics, 1964.

———. *30 Books for Teachers of English as a Foreign Language.* Washington, Center for Applied Linguistics, 1963.

———, and Lois McArdle. *A Survey of Twelve University Programs for the Preparation of Teachers of English to Speakers of Other Languages.* Washington, Center for Applied Linguistics, 1966.

Ohio, Department of Education. *Manual for Teachers. Americanization Bulletin No. 2.* Columbus, F. J. Hearn Printing Company, 1922.

Paetow, Louis J. *The Arts Course at Medieval Universities with Special Reference to Grammar and Rhetoric.* Urbana, University of Illinois Press, 1910.

Palmer, Harold. *English Pronunciation through Questions and Answers.* Cambridge, W. Heffer and Sons, 1928.

———. *A Grammar of Spoken English.* Cambridge, W. Heffer and Sons, 1924.

———. *The Oral Method of Teaching Languages.* Yonkers-on-Hudson, New York, World Book Company, 1922.

———. *The Principles of Language Study.* London, Oxford University Press, 1964.

———. *The Scientific Study and Teaching of Languages.* London, George G. Harrap and Company, 1917.

Palsgrave, John. *L'éclaircissement de la langue française.* Paris, F. Genin, 1852.

Parker, William Riley. *The National Interest and Foreign Languages.* Washington, Department of State, 1962.

Pedersen, Holger. *The Discovery of Language: Linguistic Science in the 19th Century*. Translated by John Spargo. Bloomington, University of Indiana Press, 1931.

Pei, Mario, and Frank Gaynor. *Dictionary of Linguistics*. New York, Philosophical Library, 1954.

Pincas, Anita. "Structural Linguistics and Systematic Composition Teaching to Students of English as a Foreign Language," *Language Learning*, Vol. XII, No. 3 (1962), 185–94.

Politzer, Robert L. *Foreign Language Learning. A Linguistic Introduction. Preliminary Edition*. Englewood Cliffs, New Jersey, Prentice-Hall, 1965.

———. "The Impact of Linguistics on Language Teaching: Past, Present, Future," *Modern Language Journal*, March, 1964, pp. 146–51.

———. "Pattern Practice for Reading," *Language Learning*, Vol. XIV, Nos. 3–4 (1964), 127–35.

Pooley, Robert. *Teaching English Grammar*. New York, Appleton-Century-Crofts, 1957.

Priestly, Joseph. *The Rudiments of English Grammar*. London, J. and F. Rivington, 1772.

Principles of the International Phonetic Association. London, International Phonetic Association, 1949.

Quick, Robert H. *Essays on Educational Reformers*. New York, D. Appleton and Company, 1902.

Quintilian. *Quintilian's Institutes of Oratory: or Education of an Orator*. Translated by John Selby Watson. Vol. I. London, George Bell and Sons, 1887.

Quirk, Randolph, ed. *The Teaching of English*. London, Oxford, 1964.

Reaman, George E. "A Method of Teaching English to Foreigners." Unpublished Ph.D. dissertation, Cornell University, 1921.

Rehder, Helmut, and W. Freeman Twaddell. "A.S.T.P. at Wisconsin," *German Quarterly*, Vol. XVII, No. 4, Part I (November, 1944), 216–23.

Research Club in Language Learning. *Selected Articles from Language Learning, Series I*. Ann Arbor, University of Michigan Press, 1953.

———. *Theory and Practice in English as a Foreign Language. Selected Articles from Language Learning, No. 2*. Ann Arbor, University of Michigan Press, 1963.

Rice, Frank, ed. *Study of the Role of Second Languages in Asia, Africa and Latin America.* Washington, Center for Applied Linguistics, 1962.

Richardson, Ethel. *Immigrant Education Manual. Bulletin No. 5A,* Superintendent of Public Instruction. Sacramento, California, State Printing Office, 1922.

Roberts, Paul. *Understanding English.* New York, Harper and Row, 1958.

Roberts, Peter. *The Problem of Americanization.* New York, Macmillan, 1920.

Robins, R. H. *Ancient and Medieval Grammatical Theory.* London, G. Bell and Sons, 1951.

————. *General Linguistics: An Introductory Survey.* London, Longmans, Green, 1964.

Sandy, John E. *A History of Classical Scholarship.* Vol. I. Cambridge, at the University Press, 1921.

Sapir, Edward. *Language: An Introduction to the Study of Speech.* New York, Harcourt, Brace and Company, 1921.

————. "Sound Patterns in Language," *Language,* Vol. I, No. 2 (1925), 37–51.

Sasnett, Martena Tenney, ed. *A Guide to the Admission and Placement of Foreign Students.* New York, Institute of International Education, 1962.

Saussure, Ferdinand de. *Course in General Linguistics.* Edited by Charles Bally and Albert Sechehaye. Translated by Wade Baskin. New York, Philosophical Library, 1959.

Sauveur, Lambert. *Introduction to the Teaching of Living Languages without Grammar or Dictionary.* Boston, Schoenhof and Moeller, 1875.

Scott, Charles T. "Literature and EFL Program," *Modern Language Journal,* Vol. XLVIII, No. 8 (December, 1964), 489–93.

Shen, Yao, and Ruth H. Crymes. *Teaching English as a Second Language: A Classified Bibliography.* Honolulu, East-West Center Press, 1965.

Sledd, James, and Gwin J. Kolb. *Dr. Johnson's Dictionary.* Chicago, University of Chicago Press, 1955.

Bibliography

Smail, William M. *Quintilian on Education.* Oxford, Clarendon Press, 1938.

Smith, Henry L. *Linguistic Science and the Teaching of English.* Cambridge, Harvard University Press, 1956.

Smith, Roswell. *English Grammar on the Productive System.* Philadelphia, Marshall, Williams, and Butler, 1841.

Stack, Edward. *The Language Laboratory and Modern Language Teaching.* New York, Oxford University Press, 1960.

Stevick, Earl, Marianne Lehr, and Paul Imhoff, eds. *An Active Introduction to Swahili: Geography.* Washington, Foreign Service Institute, 1966.

"Survey of Programs in English as a Second Language at the Intermediate and Advanced Levels, Prepared for the Association of Teachers of English as a Second Language, NAFSA." Survey Committee, University of Illinois, 1967.

Sweet, Henry. *A Handbook of Phonetics.* Oxford, Clarendon Press, 1877.

―――. *The Practical Study of Languages: A Guide for Teachers and Learners.* London, J. M. Dent and Sons, 1926.

―――. *A Primer of Spoken English.* Oxford, Clarendon Press, 1895.

Swinton, William. *Language Lessons.* New York, Harper, 1876.

Talbot, Winthrop. *Teaching English to Aliens: A Bibliography. Bulletin No. 39,* U.S. Bureau of Education. Washington, 1917.

Thompson, Frank V. *Schooling of the Immigrant.* New York, Harper and Sons, 1920.

Trager, George L., and Henry Lee Smith, *An Outline of English Structure.* Washington, American Council of Learned Societies, 1957.

Trubetzkoy, Nicholai. "La phonologie actuelle," *Journal de Psychologie,* XXXᵉ année, Nos. 1–4 (January 15–April 15, 1933), 227–46.

United States, Army Service Forces. Army Specialized Training Division. *Essential Facts About the ASTP.* Washington, U.S. Government Printing Office, 1943.

United States, Bureau of the Census. *Abstract of the fourteenth census of the United States, 1920.* Washington, Government Printing Office, 1923.

―――. *Abstract of the twelfth census of the United States, 1900.* Washington, Government Printing Office, 1902.

———. *Fifteenth Census of the United States; Abstract of the Fifteenth Census.* Washington, Government Printing Office, 1933.

———. *Fourteenth census of the United States taken in the year 1920.* Washington, Government Printing Office, 1921–23.

United States, Bureau of Education. *Methods of Teaching Adult Aliens and Native Illiterates. Bulletin No. 7,* U.S. Bureau of Education. Washington, 1927.

———. *Proceedings Americanization Conference.* Washington, U.S. Government Printing Office, 1919.

United States, Department of Justice. *Educational Institutions Approved by Attorney General.* Washington, U.S. Government Printing Office, 1941.

University of the State of New York. *Organization of Schools in English for the Foreign-Born.* Albany, State Department of Education, 1919.

Valdman, Albert, ed. *Trends in Language Teaching.* New York, McGraw-Hill Book Company, 1966.

Valverde, Luis James. "Multi-Disciplinary Bases for the Teaching-Learning of English as a Second Language." Unpublished Ph.D. dissertation, University of California at Los Angeles, 1960.

Walker, Elna LaVerne. "Teaching English as a Second Language to Spanish-Speaking Adults." Unpublished Ph.D. dissertation, University of Texas, 1963.

Waterman, John T. *Perspectives in Linguistics.* Chicago, University of Chicago Press, 1963.

Watts, George B. "The Teaching of French in the United States: A History," *French Review,* Vol. XXXII, No. I (October, 1963).

Weinreich, Uriel. *Languages in Contact. Findings and Problems.* New York, Linguistic Circle of New York, 1953.

Wells, William H. *A Grammar of the English Language.* New York, Huntington and Savage, 1847.

West, Michael. *A General Service List of Words.* London, Longmans Green, 1953.

———. *Language in Education.* London, Longmans Green and Company, 1932.

Wheeler, W. Reginald, Henry King, and Alexander Davidson. *The Foreign Student in America.* New York, Association Press, 1925.

Bibliography

Whitney, William Dwight. *Sanskrit Grammar*. Cambridge, Harvard University Press, 1964.

Wilcox, Walter F. *Studies in American Demography*. Ithaca, New York, Cornell University Press, 1940.

Woodward, William H. *Desiderius Erasmus Concerning the Aim and Methods of Education*. New York, Bureau of Publications, Teachers College, Columbia, 1964.

Zeydel, Edwin H. "The Teaching of German in the United States from Colonial Times to Present," *Reports of Surveys and Studies of Modern Foreign Languages*, 285–308. New York, Modern Language Association, 1961.

List of EFL Texts

Allen, Virginia F. *People in Fact and Fiction*. New York, Thomas Y. Crowell Company, 1957.

————, and Robert L. Allen. *Review Exercises for English as a Foreign Language*. New York, Thomas Y. Crowell Company, 1961.

Austin, Ruth. *Lessons in English for Foreign Women*. New York, American Book Company, 1913.

Baumell, Dennis, and Robert Saitz. *Advanced Reading and Writing*. New York, Holt, Rinehart and Winston, 1965.

Beshgeturian, Azniv. *Foreigners' Guide to English*. Yonkers-on-Hudson, New York, World Book Company, 1914.

Bigelow, Gordon E., and David P. Harris. *The United States of America: Readings in English as a Second Language*. New York, Holt, Rinehart and Winston, 1960.

Chancellor, William E. *Reading and Language Lessons for Evening Schools*. New York, American Book Company, 1904.

Croft, Kenneth. *Reading and Word Study for Students of English as a Second Language*. Englewood Cliffs, New Jersey, Prentice-Hall, 1960.

Crowell, Thomas Lee. *A Glossary of Phrases with Prepositions*. Englewood Cliffs, New Jersey, Prentice-Hall, 1960.

Danielson, Dorothy, and Rebecca Hayden. *Reading in English*. Englewood Cliffs, New Jersey, Prentice-Hall, 1961.

Dixson, Robert. *Second Book in English*. New York, Regents Publishing Company, 1950.

———, and Isobel Y. Fisher. *Beginning Lessons in English*. New York, Regents Publishing Company, 1959.

Doty, Gladys G., and Janet Ross. *Language and Life in the U.S.A.* New York, Harper and Row, 1960.

Fuller, Helene, and Florence Wasell. *Advanced English Exercises*. New York, McGraw-Hill Book Company, 1961.

Goldberger, Henry H. *English for Coming Citizens*. New York, Charles Scribner's Sons, 1918.

———. *Second Book in English for Coming Citizens*. New York, Charles Scribner's Sons, 1921.

Hayden, Rebecca, Aurora Quiros Haggard, and Dorothy Pilgrim. *Mastering American English*. Englewood Cliffs, New Jersey, Prentice-Hall, 1956.

Houghton, Frederick. *First Lessons in English for Foreigners in Evening Schools*. New York, American Book Company, 1911.

———. *Second Book in English for Foreigners in Evening Schools*. New York, American Book Company, 1917.

Institute of Modern Languages. *American English Dialogues*. Washington, Institute of Modern Languages, 1961.

———. *American English Pronunciation Lessons*. Washington, Institute of Modern Languages, 1961.

Kaplan, Robert B. *Reading and Rhetoric*. New York, The Odyssey Press, 1963.

Lado, Robert, and Charles C. Fries. *English Pattern Practice*. Ann Arbor, University of Michigan Press, 1943.

———. *English Pronunciation*. Ann Arbor, University of Michigan Press, 1954.

———. *English Sentence Patterns*. Ann Arbor, University of Michigan Press, 1957.

———. *Lessons in Vocabulary*. Ann Arbor, University of Michigan Press, 1956.

Mintz, Frances S. *The New American Citizen*. New York, Macmillan Company, 1919.

Newmark, Leonard, Jan Ann Lawson Hinely, and Jerome Mintz. *Using American English*. New York, Harper and Row, 1965.

O'Brien, Sarah. *English for Foreigners. Book One and Book Two*. Boston, Houghton Mifflin Company, 1909.

Osman, Neile. *Modern English: A Self-Tutor or Class Text for Foreign Students.* Tokyo, Charles Tuttle Company, 1959.

Paratore, Angela. *English Exercises. English as a Foreign Language.* New York, Rinehart and Company, 1958.

Praninskas, Jean. *Rapid Review of English Grammar.* Englewood Cliffs, New Jersey, Prentice-Hall, 1957.

Prator, Clifford. *Manual of American English Pronunciation.* New York, Holt, Rinehart and Winston, 1957.

Prior, Anna, and Anna I. Ryan. *How to Learn English.* New York, Macmillan Company, 1911.

Roberts, Peter. *English for Coming Americans. Advanced Course.* New York, Associated Press, 1911, 1922.

Ross, Janet, and Gladys Doty. *Writing English.* New York, Harper and Row, 1965.

Slager, William, et al. *English for Today.* New York, McGraw-Hill Book Company, 1962.

Taylor, Grant. *American English Reader.* New York, McGraw-Hill Book Company, 1960.

———. *Learning American English.* New York, Saxon Press, 1956.

———. *Mastering American English.* New York, Saxon Press, 1956.

———. *Practicing American English.* New York, Saxon Press, 1960.

Wright, Audrey. *Practice Your English.* All English ed. New York, American Book Company, 1960.

Index

Index

The paper on which this book is printed bears the watermark of the University of Oklahoma Press and has an effective life of at least three hundred years.